VITAL RECORDS
OF
CHILMARK, MASSACHUSETTS,
TO THE YEAR 1850

ADDENDA

Provided By

Catherine Merwin Mayhew

HERITAGE
BOOKS, INC.

Copyright 1991

By Catherine Merwin Mayhew

Published 1991 By

HERITAGE BOOKS, INC.
1540E Pointer Ridge Place, Bowie, Maryland 20716
(301) 390-7709

ISBN 1-55613-543-2

A Complete Catalog Listing Hundreds of Titles on
History, Genealogy & Americana
Free on Request

VITAL RECORDS

OF

CHILMARK,

MASSACHUSETTS,

TO THE YEAR 1850.

PUBLISHED BY THE
NEW-ENGLAND HISTORIC GENEALOGICAL SOCIETY,
AT THE CHARGE OF
THE EDDY TOWN-RECORD FUND.

BOSTON, MASS.,
1904.

THIS publication is issued under the authority of a vote passed by the NEW-ENGLAND HISTORIC GENEALOGICAL SOCIETY, 6 November, 1901, as follows:

Voted: That the sum of $20,000, from the bequest of the late Robert Henry Eddy, be set aside as a special fund to be called the Eddy Town-Record Fund, for the sole purpose of publishing the Vital Records of the towns of Massachusetts, and that the Council be authorized and instructed to make such arrangements as may be necessary for such publication. And the treasurer is hereby instructed to honor such drafts as shall be authorized by the Council for this purpose.

Committee on Publications.

C. B. TILLINGHAST, FRANCIS EVERETT BLAKE,
CHARLES KNOWLES BOLTON, DON GLEASON HILL,
EDMUND DANA BARBOUR.

Editor.
HENRY ERNEST WOODS.

Stanhope Press
F. H. GILSON COMPANY
BOSTON, U.S.A.

THE TOWN OF CHILMARK, County of Dukes County, was established September 14, 1694, from common land.

October 30, 1714, "the Mannour of Tisbury, commonly called Chilmark," to have all the powers of a town.

Population by census: 1765 (Prov.), 663; 1776 (Prov.), 769; 1790 (U.S.), 771; 1800 (U.S.), 800; 1810 (U.S.), 723; 1820 (U.S.), 695; 1830 (U.S.), 691; 1840 (U.S.), 702; 1850 (U.S.), 747; 1855 (State), 676; 1860 (U.S.), 654; 1865 (State), 548; 1870 (U.S.), 476; 1875 (State), 508; 1880 (U.S.), 494; 1885 (State), 412; 1890 (U.S.), 353; 1895 (State), 304; 1900 (U.S.), 324.

EXPLANATIONS.

1. WHEN places other than Chilmark and Massachusetts are named in the original records, they are given in the printed copy.

2. In all records the original spelling is followed.

3. The various spellings of a name should be examined, as items about the same family or individual might be found under different spellings.

4. Marriages and intentions of marriages are printed under the names of both parties, but the full information concerning each party is given only in the entry under his or her name. When both the marriage and intention of marriage are recorded, only the marriage record is printed; and where a marriage appears without the intention recorded, it is designated with an asterisk.

5. Additional information which does not appear in the original text of an item, i.e., any explanation, query, inference, or difference shown in other entries of the record, is bracketed. Parentheses are used only when they occur in the original text, or to separate clauses found there — such as the birth-place of parents, in late marriage records.

ABBREVIATIONS.

a. — age
abt. — about
b. — born
ch. — child
chn. — children
Co. — county
d. — daughter; died; day
Dea. — deacon
dup. — duplicate entry
G.R. — gravestone record
h. — husband
hrs. — hours
inf. — infant
int. — publishment of intention of marriage
Jr. — junior
m. — married; month
prob. — probably
rec. — recorded
s. — son
Sr. — senior
w. — wife; week
wid. — widow
widr. — widower
y. — year
1st. — first
2d. — second
3d. — third

CHILMARK BIRTHS.

CHILMARK BIRTHS.

To the year 1850.

ADAM (see Adams), ———, d. Moses, Nov. 8, 1808.
ADAMS (see Adam), Abigirl, ch. Capt. Mayhew and Rebeccah, Aug. 11, 1760.
David Blake, s. David L. and Phebe, Aug. 20, 1843.
Dinah, ch. Capt. Mayhew and Rebeccah, Apr. 21, 1772.
Edward R., Mar. 6, 1842. G.R.
Elishab, ch. Capt. Mayhew and Rebeccah, Sept. 15, 1751.
Elizabeth, ch. Capt. Mayhew and Rebeccah, May 6, 1774.
G. Washington, s. William, July 8, 1808.
James, ch. Capt. Mayhew and Rebeccah, Sept. 30, 1754.
Love, ch. Capt. Mayhew and Rebeccah, May 6, 1764.
Mary, ch. Capt. Mayhew and Rebeccah, Mar. 31, 1769.
Mary C., Oct. 24, 1815. G.R.
Mayhew, s. Elishib and Reliance, Dec. 22, 1729.
Mayhew, ch. Capt. Mayhew and Rebeccah, Mar. 11, 1759.
Moses, ch. Capt. Mayhew and Rebeccah, Dec. 5, 1762.
Moses, Capt. [h. Susan W.], Nov. 5, 1803. G.R.
Oliver, ch. Capt. Mayhew and Rebeccah, Mar. 5, 1767.
Parnal, ch. Capt. Mayhew and Rebeccah, Dec. 15, 1757.
Rebecca, ch. Capt. Mayhew and Rebeccah, Aug. 18, 1756.
Reliance, ch. Capt. Mayhew and Rebeccah, Nov. 5, 1752.
Susan Redfield, d. David L. and Phebe Mayhew, Apr. 10, 1844.
Susannah, ch. Capt. Mayhew and Rebeccah, Aug. 31, 1765.
William, ch. Capt. Mayhew and Rebeccah, Aug. 15, 1770.
———, d. Calvin C. and Lydia, Mar. 10, 1844.
———, d. David and Phebe, May 20, 1845.
———, s. Calvin C. and Lydia, Sept. 4, 1846.

ALLEN, Abigail [ch. John and Margaret], July 21, 1726.
Abigail, ch. James and Abigail, Oct. —, 1757.
Abigal [ch. Eben[ezer] and Rebeckah], May 3, 1709.
Abigall 2d (Allene) [ch. Eben[ezer] and Rebeckah], May 20, 1711.

CHILMARK BIRTHS.

ALLEN, Adolphus, s. James Jr., Feb. 23, 1806.
Anthony, s. James and Abigal, Oct. 30, 1744.
Bartlet, ch. William and Love, Aug. 25, 1781.
Bartlett, s. Matthew and Temperance, Sept. 16, 1799.
Benjamin, [twin] s. Eben[ez]er and Rebeccah, Nov. 3, 1718.
Betsy, ch. Robert and Desire, May 7, 1776.
Beulah [———], w. Dea. Ezra, Feb. 26, 1769. G.R.
Bulah, ch. Samuel and Bulah, Jan. 31, 1756.
Bulah D., ch. Ephrain and Rebecca, Aug. 29, 1811.
Cathrine, ch. Ephraim and Hannah, Oct. 13, 1768.
Charles, ch. Ephrain and Rebecca, June 6, 1822.
Clarrissa (Mayhew) [w. Tristram], Dec. 8, 1770.
Clorissa, ch. Tristram and Clarrissa, Feb. 26, 1814.
David, s. William and Sarah, Feb. 11, 1741-2.
Davis, ch. Ephraim and Hannah, Aug. 29, 1778.
Deborah, d. Jonathan and Deborah, Jan. 3, 1763.
Deborah, ch. William and Love, Feb. 13, 1785.
Deborah, ch. Tristram and Clarrissa, Jan. 24, 1807.
Desire, ch. Robert and Desire, Nov. 5, 1767.
Eleazer [ch. Eben[ezer] and Rebeckah], May 16, 1706.
Eleaz[e]r, ch. John and Margaret, June 10, 1739.
Eliezer, ch. James and Abigal, Oct. —, 1754.
Elisabeth, d. Eben[ezer] and Rebeckah, Apr. 13, 1701.
Elizabeth, d. John and Margaret, Sept. 29, 1720.
Elizabeth, ch. John and Ann, Apr. 20, 1752.
Elizabeth, ch. John and Mary, Sept. 3, 1782.
Ephraim, s. Samuel and Bulah, Oct. 26, 1742.
Ephraim, ch. Ephraim and Hannah, Aug. 31, 1784.
Ephraim, ch. Ephrain and Rebecca, Mar. 2, 1820.
Ephrain [h. Rebecca], Aug. 31, 1784.
Eunice, d. Jonathan and Deborah, Dec. 24, 1772.
Ezra, ch. Robert and Desire [dup. Desier], July 5, 1755.
Frederick, s. Jonathan and Deborah, Dec. 22, 1780.
Frederick, ch. Tristram and Clarrissa, Aug. 25, 1811.
George, [twin] ch. Ephraim and Hannah, June 28, 1771.
Hannah, ch. John and Margaret, July 23, 1741.
Hannah, ch. James and Abigal, Jan. 13, 1753.
Hannah, ch. Ephraim and Hannah, Mar. 28, 1781.
Hannah M., ch. Ephrain and Rebecca, Sept. 10, 1809.
Harriet, ch. Ephrain and Rebecca, Aug. 31, 1807.
Henry, s. Jonathan and Deborah, July 29, 1777.
Homes, s. Jonathan and Deborah, Jan. 29, 1775.
Horace, ch. Sibulon and Prudence, Sept. 7, 1804.
Huldah, ch. Robert and Desire [dup. Desier], Oct. 29, 1753.

ALLEN, James, s. Eben[ezer] and Rebecca, May 8, 1716.
James, ch. Silvanus and Jane, Mar. 28, 1732.
James, ch. Dea. James and Martha, May 23, 1762.
James, s. James and Lois, Feb. 3, 1785.
Jane, d. John and Margaret, Aug. 28, 1722.
Jane, ch. Dea. James and Martha, July 2, 1759.
Jane, [twin] ch. William and Love, June 12, 1787.
Jedidah, ch. Samuel and Bulah, Sept. 20, 1752.
John, s. John and Margaret, Apr. 1, 1730.
John, ch. John and Ann, Mar. 14, 1755.
John, ch. John and Mary, Jan. 9, 1779.
John W., ch. Ephrain and Rebecca, Mar. 7, 1826.
Jonathan, s. Eben[ezer] and Rebecca, Sept. 12, 1713.
Jonathan, s. John and Margaret, Sept. 2, 1734.
Jonathan, s. Jonathan and Deborah, Mar. 8, 1771.
Jonathan, ch. Tristram and Clarrissa, Oct. 7, 1796.
Joseph, [twin] s. Eben[ez]er and Rebeccah, Nov. 3, 1718.
Joshua, ch. Sibulon and Prudence, Mar. 10, 1800.
Julia, ch. Sibulon and Prudence, Mar. 1, 1791.
Katherine, [twin] d. John and Margaret, Feb. 26, 1717.
Katherine, ch. Silvanus and Jane, Nov. 19, 1727.
Lois, ch. Robert and Desire, July 19, 1762.
Louisa [dup. Loisa], ch. Sibulon [dup. Zebulon] and Prudence, Nov. 25, 1807.
Love, [twin] ch. William and Love, June 12, 1787.
Margaret, d. John and Margaret, Sept. 17, 1724.
Margarett C., ch. Ephrain and Rebecca, July 14, 1813.
Martha [ch. Eben[ezer] and Rebeckah], Sept. 6, 1703.
Martha, ch. James and Abigal, Dec. 28, 1742.
Martha, ch. Dea. James and Martha, Apr. 14, 1767.
Mary, d. John and Margaret, Apr. 3, 1728.
Mary, ch. Silvanus and Jane, Dec. 6, 1729.
Mary, ch. John and Mary, Sept. 6, 1780.
Mary Ann, ch. Tristram and Clarrissa, Jan. 13, 1802.
Mary C., d. Matthew H. and Mary Ann, May 30, 1842.
Matthew, ch. Robert and Desire, June 7, 1773.
Mayhew, ch. James and Abigail, Mar. 24, 1760.
Molly, ch. Robert and Desire, Feb. 3, 1758.
Myra, ch. Sibulon and Prudence, Sept. 25, 1794.
Nathaniel, s. William and Sarah, Jan. 21, 1739-40.
Patience, d. Matthew and Patience, Oct. 20, 1797.
Patince [———], w. Matthew, Sept. 4, 1777.
Peggy, ch. John and Ann, Feb. 6, 1754.
Peggy, ch. Robert and Desire, Mar. 22, 1760.

ALLEN, Percy, ch. Samuel and Bulah, Sept. 13, 1747.
Persis, ch. Ephraim and Hannah, Sept. 9, 1774.
Prudence, ch. Dea. James and Martha, Mar. 9, 1778.
Prudence (Mayhew) [w. Sibulon], ———.
Rebeca, ch. Ephrain and Rebecca, Jan. 19, 1818.
Rebecca, ch. Robert and Desire, July 15, 1770.
Rebecca [———] [w. Ephrain], Apr. 17, 1782.
Rebeccah, ch. James and Abigal, May 17, 1749.
Rebeckah, [twin] d. John and Margaret, Feb. 26, 1717.
Robert, s. John and Margaret, July 20, 1732.
Robert, ch. Robert and Desire, Apr. 10, 1765.
Sally Mayhew, ch. Sibulon and Prudence, July 10, 1797.
Samuel, [twin] ch. Ephraim and Hannah, June 28, 1771.
Samuel, ch. Ephrain and Rebecca, Nov. 18, 1815.
Sarah, ch. James and Abigail, Feb. 13, 1763.
Sibulon [h. Prudence (Mayhew)], ———.
Silvanus, ch. Dea. James and Martha, Aug. 27, 1770.
Sophronia, d. Henry, Oct. 6, 1806.
Susanah, d. William and Sarah, Nov. 5, 1738.
Temprance [———], w. Matthew, Apr. 13, 1780.
Theodore, s. Jonathan and Deborah, Mar. 15, 1767.
Thomas L., ch. Tristram and Clarrissa, Feb. 8, 1799.
Tristram, s. Jonathan and Deborah, Mar. 17, 1765.
Tristram 2d [dup. omits 2d], s. Jonathan and Deborah [dup. [h. Clarrissa (Mayhew)]], Apr. 25 [dup. Apr. 24], 1769.
Tristram, ch. Tristram and Clarrissa, Sept. 5, 1804. [Tristram Jr., G.R.]
Truman, ch. William and Love, June 19, 1783.
William, s. John and Margaret, Mar. 6, 1719.
William, ch. Silvanus and Jane, Oct. 4, 1735.
William, s. William and Sarah, June 20, 1745.
William, ch. Dea. James and Martha, Jan. 5, 1756.
William, ch. William and Love, Apr. 16, 1780.
Zach[eu]s, s. William and Sarah, Feb. 4, 1744–5.
Zebulon, ch. Dea. James and Martha, Nov. 27, 1764.
Zebulon, see Sibulon.
———, s. Matthew W. and Mary Ann, Aug. 20, 1845.

AUSTIN, Joseph, Sept. 14, 1813. G.R.
———, s. Joseph and Averlina, Apr. — [1849].

BASSET (see Bassett, Bassitt), Nathan, s. Nathan and Mary, Feb. 14, 1701–2.

BASSETT (see Basset, Bassitt), Anna, ch. Samuel and Anna, Mar. 22, 1787.
Anna, ch. William and Olivia, July 8, 1803.
Asahel, ch. Ebenezer and Ab[i]gail, Nov. 26, 1780.
Baraciah [dup. Barakiah Basset], ch. Nathan and Mary, Mar. 2, 1704.
Benjamin, s. John and Jean, July 21, 1752.
Carrissa [———] [w. Norton], Mar. 23, 1772.
Charlotte Hillman, d. Nathan and Deborah Norton, Feb. 29, 1848.
Clement, ch. Nathan and Marcy, Apr. 17, 1768.
Cornelious, ch. Fortunatus and Sarah, Oct. 6, 1778.
Cornelus, ch. Nathan and Mary, Apr. 21, 1695.
Elisabeth, d. John and Jean, May 16, 1736.
Elishab Adams, ch. Ebenezer and Ab[i]gail, July 22, 1785.
Elizabath [dup. Elizabeth Bassitt], d. Benjamin and Abigail, June 13, 1780.
Elizabeth, ch. Nathan and Mary, Sept. 12, 1699.
Elizabeth, ch. Samuel and Anna, June 8, 1785.
Ephream Guld, ch. Samuel and Anna, May 7, 1780.
Fanny (Tillton) [w. Norton Jr.], Aug. 22, 1802. [w. Norton, G.R.]
Fortunatus, ch. Fortunatus and Sarah, June 30, 1775.
Henry, ch. John and Anna, Aug. 19, 1785.
Hephzibath, ch. Samuel and Anna, Sept. 13, 1783.
Hope, ch. Nathan and Mary, July 26, 1708.
James, ch. John and Anna, May 13, 1783.
Jane, ch. Joseph and Mary, Dec. 25, 1784.
Jedidah, d. William and Ann, July 17, 1749.
John, s. Nathan and Mary, Apr. 25, 1706.
John, ch. Joseph and Mary, June 2, 1786.
John Norton, ch. John and Anna, Aug. 4, 1780.
Jonathan, s. John and Jean, Aug. 13, 1741.
Joseph, s. John and Jean, Apr. 26, 1743.
Joseph, ch. Joseph and Mary, Sept. 15, 1788.
Katharine, d. Nath[anie]l and Katharine, Mar. 26, 1795.
Lydia, ch. Nathan and Marcy, Aug. 18, 1766.
Lydia Norton, ch. Samuel and Anna, Apr. 28, 1789.
Martha, ch. Silas and Jane, Aug. 22, 1780.
Martha, ch. Norton and Carrissa, Aug. 29, 1792, in N.Y. [written in pencil].
Martha G. [ch. Norton Jr. and Fanny] [dup. [w. William Norton]], Apr. 7, 1825.
Mary, ch. Nathan and Mary, May 10, 1697.

BASSETT, Mary, ch. William and Olivia, Aug. 16, 1801.
Mary T. [ch. Norton Jr. and Fanny], Oct. 19, 1827.
Mayhew, ch. Joseph and Mary, Sept. 21, 1792.
Nathan, ch. William and Olivia, Aug. 4, 1795.
Nathan S., ch. Norton and Carrissa, Dec. 20, 1796, in N.Y. [written in pencil].
Nathaniel, ch. Nathan and Mary, Aug. 2, 1715.
Nathaniel, s. William and Anna, Nov. 16, 1727.
Nathaniel, s. Nathaniel and Katharine, June 2, 1789.
Norton [h. Carrissa], May 22, 1770.
Norton [dup. Jr.], ch. Norton and Carrissa [dup. [h. Fanny (Tillton)]], Sept. 7, 1794, in N.Y. [written in pencil].
Norton, s. Nathan S. and Deborah, Apr. 12, 1844.
Peres, ch. Nathan and Marcy, May 12, 1764.
Perez, ch. William and Olivia, June 1, 1797.
Peter Norton, ch. Ebenezer and Ab[i]gail, Dec. 16, 1782.
Polly, ch. Nathan and Marcy, June 28, 1773.
Ruth, ch. Nathan and Mary, Feb. 17, 1691.
Ruth, d. John and Jean, June 17, 1738.
Samuel, ch. Nathan and Mary, Feb. 4, 1693.
Samuel, ch. Cornelious and Lydia, Mar. 18, 1749.
Samuel, ch. Samuel and Anna, Dec. 1, 1781.
Sarah, ch. Cornelious and Lydia, Jan. 13, 1747.
Sarah, ch. Ebenezer and Ab[i]gail, May 7, 1787.
Silas, s. John and Jean, Aug. 9, 1746.
Silas, ch. Joseph and Mary, July 11, 1790.
William, ch. Nathan and Mary, Dec. 17, 1702.
William, ch. Nathan and Marcy, May 25, 1770.
William, ch. Fortunatus and Sarah, July 11, 1772.
――――, s. Norton Jr. and Fanny, Feb. 22, 1824.

BASSITT (see Basset, Bassett), Abigail (Nickerson) [w. Benjamin], Nov. 22, 1754.
Abigail [dup. Bassett], ch. Benjamin and Abigail, June 28, 1784. [Bassett, G.R.]
Benjamin [h. Abigail (Nickerson)], Aug. 1, 1752.
Benjamin [dup. Bassett], ch. Benjamin and Abigail, Oct. 21 [dup. Oct. 2], 1787.
Jonathan [dup. Bassett], ch. Benjamin and Abigail, Mar. 20, 1792.
Ruth [dup. Bassett], ch. Benjamin and Abigail, Sept. 4, 1789.
Zipporah [dup. Bassett], ch. Benjamin and Abigail, June 18, 1782. [Ziphorah Bassett, d. Benjamin Esq. and Abigail, G.R.]

CHILMARK BIRTHS.

BOARDMAN, Abigail, ch. Rev. Andrew and Katharine, Apr. 9, 1750.
Andrew Jr., ch. Rev. Andrew and Katharine, July 16, 1748.
Elizabeth, ch. Rev. Andrew and Katharine, Nov. 25, 1755.
Herbert, ch. Rev. Andrew and Katharine, Apr. 11, 1764.
Jane, ch. Rev. Andrew and Katharine, Aug. 14, 1767.
Katharine Jr., ch. Rev. Andrew and Katharine, Mar. 19, 1752.
Sylv[anu]s, ch. Rev. Andrew and Katharine, Sept. 15, 1757.
Walter, ch. Rev. Andrew and Katharine, July 12, 1761.
William, ch. Rev. Andrew and Katharine, Nov. 16, 1753.

BURGES, Mary, d. Benja[min] Jr. and Abigal, May 26, 1749.
Will[ia]m, s. Benja[min] Jr. and Abigal, May 2, 1744.

BUTLER, Constant Norton, ch. Nicholas and Lucy, Oct. 5, 1793.
Frederick Norton, ch. Nicholas and Lucy, June 10, 1791.
Jean, d. David and Anne, May 10, 1728.
Martha, d. David and Anne, May 13, 1730.
Mary, d. David and Anne, Oct. 17, 1726.
Thomas, s. David and Anne, Mar. 18, 1732.

CHACE (see Chase), Cornelos, s. Isaac and Mary, July 14, 1705.
Isaac, ch. Isaac and Mary, July 15, 1712.
Levi, ch. Isaac and Mary, Mar. 30, 1716.
Nathan, s. Isaac and Mary, July 16, 1702.
Stephen, s. Isaac and Mary, Sept. 24, 1708.

CHASE (see Chace), Joseph, ch. Isaac and Mary, Dec. 22, 1713.

CLAGHORN, Elizabeth, ch. Shobal and Expriance, Aug. 1, 1746.
Georg, ch. Shobal and Expriance, July 6, 1748.
Jeames, ch. Shobal and Expriance, June 28 [dup. June 25], 1751.

CLARK, Hannah, d. W[illia]m and Bethiah, June 19, 1723.
Jane, d. W[illia]m and Bethiah, Jan. 1, 1726.
Thankfull, d. W[illia]m and Bethiah, Aug. 7, 1724.
Will[ia]m, s. Will[ia]m and Bethiah, Apr. 15, 1716.

CLEVELAND, Sarah E. [———], w. George M., ———, 1772. G.R.

COFFIN, Love of Edgartown, May 3, 1756.

COTTLE, Abram Williams, s. William, [Sept.] 7, 1808.
Catharine, [twin] d. Abishai and Catharine, Aug. 14, 1766.
Jane [ch. Abishai and Catharine], Dec. 20, 1769.
Jerusha T., w. George W. Stuart, Oct. 22, 1805. G.R.
John [ch. Abishai and Catharine], Aug. 24, 1768.
Lidia, ch. Benjamin and Sarah, Oct. 27, 1754.
Margaret [———], w. George D., Apr. 19, 1800. G.R.
Sally Dunham, d. Mayhew, June 27, 1807.
Salome, ch. Benjamin and Sarah, May 7, 1752.
Shubal Smith (Clottle), s. Benjamin and Sarah, June 8 [? 5], 1757.
Zerviah, [twin] d. Abishai and Catharine, Aug. 14, 1766.
———, s. George D. and Peggy, July 2, 1842.

CUNINGIM, John, s. John and Catharine, June 7, 1721.

DAVIS, George H., July 3, 1822. G.R.
———, s. John and Mary Ann, May —, 1844.
———, d. John and Mary Ann, June 2, 1845.

DUNHAM, Cornelos, ch. Dan[ie]ll and Sarah, May 10, 1748.
Dan[ie]ll, ch. Dan[ie]ll and Sarah, Mar. 9, 1746.
Elezer, ch. Dan[ie]ll and Sarah, Dec. 18, 1743.
Jonathan, ch. Dan[ie]ll and Sarah, Mar. 23, 1751.
Mary, ch. Dan[ie]ll and Sarah, Mar. 30, 1756.
Sarah, ch. Dan[ie]ll and Sarah, Feb. 26, 1754.
Thankful, ch. Dan[ie]ll and Sarah, Sept. 10, 1741.
———, d. John and Nancy, Apr. 28, 1846.

FLANDERS, Agnes, d. William and Agnes, Aug. 27, 1844.
Agnes L., d. Samuel and Keziah Lumbert [dup. F.], Aug. 28, 1845.
Almira, ch. John and Hannah, Oct. 16, 1795.
Alvin, ch. John and Hannah, July 13, 1794.
Augustus Hudson, s. Henry H. and Sophronia [of] Chesborough, Sept. —, 1844.
Clarissa C., d. Samuel and Keziah Lumbert [dup. F.] of Gay Head, June 21, 1847, in Gay Head.
Cyrus H., s. Richard and Parnel Poole, Nov. 9, 1846.
Daniel, ch. John and Hannah, Nov. 6, 1801.
Daniel H., s. Daniel and Jane Mayhew, Feb. 22, 1847.
Edy C., s. Samuel and Keziah F. (Lumbert), Nov. 21, 1840.
Fannie J., d. Samuel and Keziah F. (Lumbert), Dec. 28, 1837.
Freeman B., s. Samuel and Keziah Lumbert [dup. F.] of Gay Head, Oct. 30, 1848, in Gay Head.

CHILMARK BIRTHS. 17

FLANDERS, Hannah (Tillton) [w. John], Apr. 4, 1770.
Hannah, ch. John and Hannah [dup. [w. Josiah Tillton]], Apr. 15, 1799.
John [h. Hannah (Tillton)], Sept. 14, 1769.
John, ch. John and Hannah, May 1 [? 18], 1797.
Keziah F. (Lumbert) [w. Samuel], ———.
Olivia F. [dup. T.], d. Samuel and Keziah F. (Lumbert), Aug. 29, 1842.
Otis Smith, s. Daniel and Charlote, Aug. 12, 1842.
Rebecca, ch. John and Hannah [dup. [w. Leonard West]], June 29, 1806.
Richard, ch. John and Hannah, Mar. 29, 1803.
Samuel, ch. John and Hannah [dup. [h. Keziah F. (Lumbert)]], June 4, 1810.
Wilbur F., s. Samuel and Keziah F. (Lumbert), Jan. 30, 1839.
William, Capt., Jan. 13, 1812. G.R.
William, ch. John and Hannah, Jan. 13, 1813.
———, d. John, June 29, 1806.
———, d. Daniel and Jane, Apr. 21, 1844.

FULLER, Anna, ch. Rev. Timothy and Sarah, May 15, 1780.
Timothy, ch. Rev. Timothy and Sarah, July 11, 1778.

GOFF, Ann, d. William and Lydia S., Feb. 20, 1846.
Robert, s. William and Lydia, Aug. 16, 1844.
William Albert, s. William and Lydia, June — [1848].

GOULD, Cecila, d. Horace, Feb. 3, 1806.
Ephraim, s. John and Sarah, Jan. 22, 1734.

GRAY, Sarah, d. Edward and Mary of Tiverton, Apr. 8, 1697 [see Mrs. Sarah Hunt, under Deaths]. G.R.

HACH, Joannah, d. Robert and w., Dec. 16 [dup. Dec. 6], 1753.
Prince, s. Robert, Jan. 20, 1750.

HAFFORD, Louisa P., Mar. —, 1833. G.R.

HAMMETT, Mary A. [———], w. Hiram, Aug. 26, 1824. G.R.
———, s. John and Sarah D., Apr. 18, 1844.
———, s. Hiram and Mary, Apr. — [1849].

HANCOCK, ———, d. Samuel, [Oct.] 21, 1807.
———, d. Cyrus and Thankful, Nov. — [1848].

HATCH (see Hach).

CHILMARK BIRTHS.

HILLMAN (see Hilman), Arnal, ch. Richard and Jane, Jan. 21, 1781.
Asahel, ch. Ezra and Zerniah, July 28, 1776.
Benjamin, ch. Ezra and Zerniah, Apr. 2, 1793.
Beriah, ch. Richard and Jane, Mar. 15, 1776.
Beriah T., ch. Owen Jr. and Charlotte, Jan. 28, 1843.
Betsy Chase [dup. Chace], ch. Moses and Lydia, Apr. 5, 1806.
Caroline W., ch. Owen Jr. and Charlotte, Jan. 12, 1832.
Charlotte, ch. Moses and Lydia, Jan. 7, 1803.
Charlotte J. [dup. omits J.], d. Ouen [dup. Owen] and Charlotte, May 17, 1846.
Charlotte (Tillton) (Hilliams) [w. Owen Jr.], June 8, 1804. [w. Capt. Owen, G.R.]
Clarrissa [w. Samuel Nickerson], Oct. 26, 1805.
Daniel, ch. Ezra and Zerniah, May 23, 1772.
David, ch. Benjamin and Mary, Nov. 15, 1778.
Eliphelet, ch. Richard and Jane, Feb. 20, 1786.
Fanny, ch. Moses and Lydia, Jan. 5, 1801.
Francis B. T., ch. Owen Jr. and Charlotte, Jan. 9, 1839.
Gersham, ch. Samuel and Pheba, Apr. 3, 1760.
Ihcabod, Mar. 7, 1773.
Isaiah, ch. Robert and Rebecca, June 2, 1771.
James, ch. Robert and Rebecca, Aug. 15, 1781.
Jane, ch. Samuel and Pheba, June 7, 1765.
Jane, ch. Ezra and Zerniah, Feb. 11, 1779.
Jirah, ch. Samuel and Pheba, Oct. 30, 1762.
Jirah, ch. Benjamin and Mary, Oct. 31, 1783.
Jirch, ch. Moses and Lydia, Apr. 2, 1797.
Jonathan, ch. Samuel and Pheba, Aug. 17, 1754.
Jonathan 2d [dup. Hilman, omits 2d], ch. Samuel and Pheba [dup. ch. Sam[ue]ll [and] Phebe], Sept. 6 [dup. Sept. 5], 1757.
Jonathan, ch. Robert and Rebecca, Aug. 16, 1783.
Jonathan, ch. Ezra and Zerniah, June 8, 1784.
Lydia, ch. Moses and Lydia, Dec. 3, 1804.
Mary, ch. Richard and Jane, July 9, 1784.
Matty, ch. Ezra and Zerniah, Apr. 16, 1789.
Moses, ch. Samuel and Pheba, Sept. 4, 1771.
Owen Jr. (Hilliams) [h. Charlotte (Tillton)], Jan. 19, 1804. [Capt. Owen, G.R.]
Pardon, s. Elizabeth, Oct. 15, 1787.
Parnell, ch. Samuel and Pheba, July 29, 1767.
Prince, ch. Robert and Rebecca, June 19, 1773.
Prudence, ch. Moses and Lydia, Jan. 22, 1799.

CHILMARK BIRTHS. 19

HILLMAN, Rebeca, ch. Robert and Rebecca, July 30, 1785.
Robert, ch. Benjamin and Love, Mar. 30, 1747. [Capt. Robert [h. Rebecca], G.R.]
Robert, ch. Robert and Rebecca, June 16, 1779.
Samuel, ch. Samuel and Pheba, Sept. 3, 1769.
Shadr[a]ch, ch. Ezra and Zerniah, Nov. 8, 1767.
Susanna [w. Benjamin S. Tilton], June 7, 1797.
Thankfull, ch. Richard and Jane, July 23, 1778.
Tristram, ch. Samuel and Pheba, July 16, 1752.
Tristram, ch. Moses and Lydia, Aug. 14, 1795.
Uriel, ch. Robert and Rebecca, Feb. 3, 1775.
Warren T., ch. Owen Jr. and Charlotte, Sept. 15, 1841. [Dr. Warren T., Sept. 16, G.R.]
William, ch. Benjamin and Mary, July 14, 1777.
Zachariah, s. Quen [dup. Owen] and Charlotte, Oct. — [dup. Oct. 28], 1844.
Zachariah, Oct. 16, 1845. G.R.
Zebulon, ch. Ezra and Zerniah, Apr. 4, 1786.
———, s. Mosis, Sept. 7 [?], 1808.
———, s. Owen Jr. and Charlotte, Nov. 3, 1832.
———, d. Owen Jr. and Charlotte, Jan. 16, 1836.
———, s. Owen and Charlott, Feb. 27, 1843.

HILMAN (see Hillman), Thuston, ch. Sam[ue]ll [and] Phebe, —— 16, 1752.

HOMES, Margaret (Home), d. William and Margaret, Feb. 28, 1696.

HOWLAND, Cyrus M., ch. Elijah and Sophronia, June 30, 1845. G.R.
Emma M., d. Elijah and Sophronia Tilton, Dec. 21, 1848.
William B., ch. Elijah and Sophronia, Aug. 8, 1843. G.R.
———, s. Elijah and Sophronia, Aug. 8, 1842.

JONES, Daniel, ch. Daniel and Mary, Oct. 28, 1782.
Polly, ch. Daniel and Mary, July 4, 1788.
Susanah, ch. Daniel and Mary, Apr. 22, 1778.
Thomas, ch. Daniel and Mary, Dec. 13, 1780.

LAMBERT (see Lumbert, Lumbut), Moses, Nov. 25, 1737. G.R.
Sarah, Oct. 15, 1739. G.R.

LITTLE, Mary, d. Tho[ma]s and Jedidah, Mar. 8, 1728-9.
Thomas, s. Thomas and Jedidah, July 22, 1731.

LOOK, Alfred Herbert, s. Alfred and Jane, Feb. 21, 1849.
Eunice [w. Samuel Norton], Mar. 17, 1791.
James [h. Irena W.], Apr. 25, 1806. G.R.
Moses, Jan. 7, 1791. G.R.
Prince [h. Sarah], May 10, 1750. G.R.
Prince Jr., Oct. 10, 1796. G.R.
Reuben, Jan. 15, 1789. G.R.
Sarah, July 26, 1794. G.R.
―――, d. George, Feb. 19, 1807.
―――, d. George, [Sept.] 14, 1808.

LOTHROP, Elisabeth, ch. Thomas (Lrothop) and Sarah, Sept. 13, 1768.
Peggy, ch. Thomas (Lrothop) and Sarah, Aug. 3, 1772.
Sarah, ch. Thomas (Lrothop) and Sarah, Dec. 21, 1769.
Sarson, ch. Thomas (Lrothop) and Sarah, Apr. 14, 1767.
Thomas, ch. Thomas (Lrothop) and Sarah, Jan. 22, 1771.

LUCE, Adonijah [ch. Hennery and Hannah], Aug. 15, 1717.
Eleazor, s. Hennery and Hannah, Jan. 1, 1711-12.
Johannah [ch. Hennery and Hannah], June 13, 1714.
Jonnathan [ch. Hennery and Hannah], June 15, 1722.
Robert [ch. Hennery and Hannah], Dec. 1, 1715.
―――, s. Daniel, Jan. 18, 1806.
―――, s. Daniel, May 21, 1807.
―――, s. Daniel, Dec. 5, 1808.
―――, d. Ulyssus P. and Mary, June 1, 1846.

LUMBERT (see Lambert, Lumbut), Abisha, ch. Moses (Lumbart) and Sarah, Aug. 9, 1769.
Benjamen (Lumb[e]r[t]), s. Jonathan and Rachel, July 22, 1709.
Bershaba, ch. Moses (Lumbart) and Sarah, Mar. 25, 1773.
Deborah, ch. Moses (Lumbart) and Sarah, Aug. 15, 1774.
Frederick, s. Thomas H. [and] Lydia, Sept. —, 1845.
James, ch. Moses (Lumbart) and Sarah, May 15, 1766.
Jonathan, ch. Moses (Lumbart) and Sarah, Nov. 5, 1762.
Keziah F. [w. Samuel Flanders], ―――.
Laura, ch. Moses (Lumbart) and Sarah, Feb. 15, 1776.
Marcy, ch. Moses (Lumbart) and Sarah, Mar. 6, 1765.
Melindia [Belinda], ch. Moses (Lumbart) and Sarah, Dec. 29, 1781.
Nancy, [twin] ch. Moses (Lumbart) and Sarah, Feb. 8, 1771. [Lambert, G.R.]
Peggy, [twin] ch. Moses (Lumbart) and Sarah, Feb. 8, 1771. [Lambert, G.R.]

LUMBERT, Prudence, ch. Moses (Lumbart) and Sarah, Dec. 16, 1777.
Sarah, ch. Moses (Lumbart) and Sarah, Jan. 5, 1764.
Thomas, ch. Moses (Lumbart) and Sarah, Aug. 10, 1767.
———, d. Thomas, Jan. 17, 1808.
———, s. Thomas H. and Lydia (Lumber[t]), Feb. 6, 1843.

LUMBUT (see Lambert, Lumbert), Deborah A. [———] [w. Thomas H.], ———.
Deborah T. [ch. Thomas H. and Lydia], Dec. 9, 1827.
Lydia West [ch. Thomas H. and Lydia], Aug. 23, 1829.
Lydia (West) [w. Thomas H.], ———.
Thomas G. [ch. Thomas H. and Lydia], Jan. 10, 1826.
Thomas H. [h. Deborah A.], ———. [Hon. Thomas H. Lambert, Apr. 8, 1795, G.R.]

MAC COLLUM (see McCollum), ———, d. Archable, Apr. 28, 1806.

MAGEE, Mary, d. Tho[ma]s and Mary, Oct. 12, 1727.

MANTER, Granville S., s. Granville and Catherine, Apr. 4, 1845.
———, s. Granville and Catharine Mayhew, Apr. —, 1844.
———, s. Granville and Catharine, Jan. 15 [1848].

MAYHEW, Abby J., d. Josiah and Eliza, June ——— [rec. May 25, 1848].
Abiah, d. Zephaniah and Bethiah, ——— 3, 1712–13.
Abigal, d. Experience and Remember, May 6, 1714.
Abigirl, ch. Nathan and Susanah, May 4, 1764.
Abishai, s. Math[e]w and Mary, Apr. 5, 1746.
Abner [h. Martha], Jan. 26, 1750. G.R.
Abner, s. Joseph and Deidama, Jan. 15, 1848.
Adonijah [ch. Zephaniah and Bethiah], Oct. 18, 1713.
Adonijah, ch. Zephaniah [dup. Zepeniah] and Hannah, July 20, 1736.
Alfred, Jan. 30, 1805. G.R.
Allen, s. M[atthe]w and Mary, June 18, 1767.
Andrew Boardman [ch. Nathan and Abigail], Sept. 9, 1791.
Anna, ch. Simon [and] Abiah, Mar. 24, 1760.
Anne, d. Elijah and Eunice, Mar. 9, 1729–30.
Bartlett, Rev., Aug. 11, 1829. G.R.
Benjamin, s. Benjamin and Hannah, May 21, 1717.
Benjamin, s. Benjamin and Sarah, Apr. 27, 1744.
Benjamin, s. Benjamin and Lydia, Feb. 8, 1785.

CHILMARK BIRTHS.

MAYHEW, Benjamin S., s. Benjamin and Hannah, Sept. 16, 1846.
Bershaba [ch. Benja[min] and Hannah], June 11, 1709.
Bethia, d. Matthew and Mary, Mar. 5, 1686.
Bethiah [ch. Zephaniah and Bethiah], May 20, 1723.
Bethyah [ch. Pain and Mary], Mar. 31, 1712.
Caroline [———], w. William, Sept. 4, 1800. G.R.
Caroline, ch. Allen and Unice, Sept. —, 1800 [written in pencil].
Charlotte J. [———], w. John Wesley, May 17, 1846. G.R.
Clarinda [ch. Nathan and Abigail], July 29, 1787.
Clarissa [dup. Clarrissa], d. M[atthe]w and Mary [dup. [w. Tristram Allen]], Dec. 8, 1770.
Constant, s. Elijah and Eunice, Nov. 27, 1731.
Constant, ch. Pain and Margarit, Oct. 17, 1759.
Cynthia E., d. Oliver and Hannah, Jan. 23, 1848.
David, ch. Ephraim and Jedidah, Sept. 4, 1779.
David W., s. Smith and Thankful V. (Cottle), June 18, 1832.
Davis, ch. Zachariah Jr. and Ann, Oct. 24, 1782.
Elenor, ch. Thomas and Lydia, Dec. 8, 1746.
Elizabeth, d. Pain and Dinah, Nov. 27, 1725.
Elizabeth, ch. Zachariah and Elizabeth, Jan. 30, 1749 "old stile."
Elizabeth, d. M[atthe]w and Mary, Jan. 30, 1754 "New Stile."
Elizabeth, d. Zach[eu]s and Rebeckah, Apr. 9, 1755.
Elizabeth, ch. William and Peggy, Feb. 5, 1781.
Elizabeth, d. Nathan and Abigail, July 2, 1785.
Elizebeth, ch. Thomas Waide and Parnal, Jan. 8, 1793.
Ephraim, ch. Ephraim and Jedidah, Mar. 19, 1778.
Eunice (see Unice).
Experience, Rev., A. M., Feb. 5, 1673 "N. S." G.R.
Frebon, ch. Pain and Margarit, Aug. 25, 1758.
George S., s. Joseph Jr. and Deidamia, Feb. 20, 1845.
Gilbert, ch. Jonathan and Parnal, Aug. 25, 1800.
Hannah [ch. Benja[min] and Hannah], Oct. 14, 1711.
Hannah, d. Pain and Mary, Mar. 31, 1713–14.
Hannah, d. Pain and Mary, Aug. 12, 1715.
Hannah, ch. Ephraim and Jedidah, July 7, 1794.
Hannah S., d. Elijah L. and Aseneth, Feb. — [? 1847].
Harriot, ch. Thomas Waide and Parnal, Aug. 23, 1787.
Harrison [ch. Matthew and Rebecca], ———.
Heberon, ch. Nathan and Susanah, Feb. 16, 1767.
Hebron, ch. Hebron and Deborah, July 5, 1793.
Henry S., s. Smith and Thankful Cottle, Oct. 2, 1847.
Herman, s. Ephraim and Lucinda, June 17, 1843.
Hillyard, [twin] ch. Ephraim and Jedidah, Mar. 19, 1791.
Homes, ch. Willmott and Nancey, Aug. 24, 1787.

CHILMARK BIRTHS.   23

MAYHEW, James, ch. Nathan and Susanah, Apr. 16, 1762.
James, ch. Zachariah Jr. and Ann, July 23, 1785.
James [ch. Nathan and Abigail], Oct. 16, 1789.
Jane Ann Swett, w. Edward, June 7, 1822. G.R.
Jane S. [———], w. Jonathan, Mar. 17, 1819. G.R.
Jean, ch. Simon [and] Abiah [dup. Milda], Feb. 2, 1749.
Jeane, ch. Simon and Ruth, Sept. 13, 1713.
Jedidah, d. Zephaniah and Bethiah, Apr. 18, 1719.
Jedidah, ch. Thomas and Lydia, Feb. —, 1733.
Jedidah, ch. Ephraim and Jedidah, Sept. 7, 1782.
Jemimah, d. Benja[min] and Hannah, June 14, 1707.
Jeremiah, [twin] ch. Ephraim and Jedidah, Mar. 19, 1791.
Jerusha, d. Zephaniah and Bethiah, Apr. 8, 1717.
Jerusha, ch. Zephaniah and Hannah, Dec. 13, 1743.
John, s. John and Ruth, Mar. 7, 1736.
John Wesley [h. Charlotte J.], Oct. 9, 1833. G.R.
Jonathan, ch. Zachariah and Elizabeth, Jan. 7, 1755 "New S^t."
Jonathan, ch. Jonathan and Parnal, Apr. 7, 1797.
Joseph, ch. Simon and Ruth, Feb. 26, 1709-10.
Joseph B., s. Joseph and Deidamia, Apr. 19, 1842.
Julius, s. Matthew and Rebecca, ——— [? b. after ch. b. Feb. 13, 1786].
Lemuel, ch. Thomas Waide and Parnal, May 23, 1791
Lucinda, ch. Zephaniah and Hannah, Feb. 16, 1738.
Lucinda [———], w. Ephraim, June 13, 1817. G.R.
Lucy, d. Zacheus and Susanna, July 4, 1716.
Lucy, d. Zach[eu]s and Rebekah, Apr. 25, 1753.
Lucy Look, d. Josiah and Eliza L., Apr. 11, 1844.
Luria, d. Nathan and Abigail, Sept. 18, 1782.
Lydia, d. John and Ruth, June 9, 1741.
Lydia [ch. Benjamin and Lydia], Nov. 16, 1787.
Lydia R., d. Josiah and Eliza L., Mar. 20, 1846.
Malatiah, s. Josiah and Eliza L., Dec. 4, 1848.
Maltiah, s. John and Ruth, Sept. 24, 1731.
Marinda J., d. Ephraim and Lucinda, Aug. 10, 1846.
Martha, d. Pain and Mary, Feb. 20, 1705-6.
Martha, d. M[atthe]w and Mary, Sept. 28, 1752.
Martha, ch. William and Peggy, Sept. 21, 1775.
Martha, ch. Thomas Waide and Parnal, May 7, 1789.
Martha [twin ch. Matthew and Rebecca], ———.
Mary, d. Matthew and Mary, May 25, 1680.
Mary, d. Pain and Mary, Sept. 26, 1700.
Mary, d. Zeph[aniah] and Bethiah, Apr. 3, 1721.
Mary, d. John and Ruth, May 22, 1734.

CHILMARK BIRTHS.

MAYHEW, Mary, d. Matthew and Mary, May 31, 1750.
Mary, ch. Nathan and Susanah, Mar. 10, 1774.
Mary, d. Matthew Jr. and Rebecca, Jan. 22, 1780.
Mary E. [———], w. Oliver, Nov. 16, 1822. G.R.
Mary H., d. Smith and Thankful V. (Cottle), Aug. 6, 1842.
Matilda [dup. Milda], ch. Simon [and] Abiah [dup. Milda], Aug. 22, 1751.
Matthew, s. Matthew and Mary, Nov. 29, 1674.
Matthew, s. Pain and Mary, May 15, 1721.
Matthew, s. M[atthe]w and Mary, Aug. 1, 1756.
Matthew, s. Matthew and Rebecca, Dec. 29, 1784.
Mercy [ch. Zephaniah and Bethiah], July 22, 1725.
Mira, ch. Hebron and Deborah, Apr. 9, 1798.
Moses Adams, ch. Thomas Waide and Parnal, Dec. 23, 1795.
Nathan, s. Experience and Remember, Oct. 8, 1712.
Nathan, ch. Zachariah and Elizabeth, May 18, 1741 "old stile."
Nathan, ch. Nathan and Susanah, Dec. 23, 1778.
Nathan, ch. Hebron and Deborah, Oct. 9, 1795.
Nathaniall, s. Zach[eu]s and Rebeckah, Apr. 16, 1761.
Octavus C., s. Joseph and Deidamia, Sept. 11, 1840.
Olive, d. Zach[eu]s and Rebeckah, Mar. 1, 1766.
Oliver, ch. Simon [and] Abiah, June 7, 1763.
Pain, s. Matthew and Mary, Oct. 31, 1677.
Pain, s. Pain and Mary, Jan. 19, 1701-2.
Pain, ch. Thomas and Lydia, Mar. 16, 1734.
Parnel, d. M[atthe]w and Mary, May 23, 1761.
Parnel, ch. Thomas Waide and Parnal, Sept. 23, 1785.
Peggy, d. Matthew and Mary, Dec. 19, 1747.
Peggy [twin ch. Matthew and Rebecca], ———.
Persis, ch. Simon [and] Abiah, Oct. 6, 1755.
Philip S., ch. Ephraim and Jedidah, July 13, 1797.
Prudence, d. M[atthe]w and Mary, Apr. 12, 1764.
Prudence [w. Sibulon Allen], ———.
Rebeca, ch. Jonathan and Parnal, June 18, 1795.
Rebecakah, d. Zach[eu]s and Rebeckah, Aug. 15, 1763.
Rebecca, d. Pain and Dinah, May 27, 1730.
Rebecca, d. Matthew and Rebecca, Feb. 13, 1786.
Rebeckah, d. M[atthe]w and Mary, July 12, 1774.
Rebekah, ch. Zachariah and Elizabeth, Dec. 6, 1765.
Ruth, d. Benjamin and Hannah, July 29, 1714.
Ruth, ch. Simon and Ruth, Dec. 26, 1721.
Ruth, d. John and Ruth, May 17, 1746.
Sam[ue]ll, ch. Simon and Ruth, Mar. 10, 1712-13.
Sarah, d. Pain and Mary, Aug. 7, 1708.

CHILMARK BIRTHS.

MAYHEW, Sarah, ch. Thomas and Lydia, Nov. 18, 1735.
Sarah, d. M[atthe]w and Mary, Dec. 9, 1758.
Simon, ch. Simon and Ruth, Oct. 20, 1719.
Simon, ch. Simon [and] Abiah [dup. Milda], Nov. 15, 1753.
Smith, ch. Ephraim and Jedidah, Sept. 23, 1788.
Susanah, d. Zach[eu]s and Rebecakah, June 21, 1751.
Susanna, d. Zacheus and Susanna, Nov. 5, 1714.
Susannah, ch. Nathan and Susanah, Dec. 22, 1771.
Susannah, d. Matthew and Rebecca, Nov. 7, 1782.
Theodore Allen, ch. Allen and Unice, Jan. 4, 1797.
Thomas, s. Matthew and Mary, May 5, 1683.
Thomas, s. Pain and Mary, Apr. 23, 1710.
Thomas, ch. Zephaniah and Hannah, Mar. 2, 1749.
Thomas, ch. Thomas and Lydia, Mar. 24, 1750.
Thomas Wade, s. Zach[eu]s and Rebeckah, Mar. 14, 1757.
Thomas Waid, ch. Thomas Waide and Parnal, Apr. 14, 1783.
Timothy, ch. Simon and Ruth, June 25, 1711.
Tristram, ch. Ephraim and Jedidah, Dec. 23, 1786.
Tristram [h. Jane N.], Oct. 18, 1810. G.R.
Unice, d. Exp[erience] and Remember, Apr. 4, 1716.
Wadsworth, ch. Zephaniah and Hannah, Apr. 27, 1741.
William, ch. Zachariah and Elizabeth, July 7, 1746 "old stile."
William, ch. Pain and Margarit, Jan. —, 1761.
William, ch. Nathan and Susanah, July 30, 1769.
William, ch. Ephraim and Jedidah, Dec. 11, 1784.
W[illia]m B., s. William B., Mar. 10, 1806.
Will[ia]m Brandon, ch. William and Peggy, Dec. 17, 1777.
Willmott, ch. Pain and Margarit, Aug. 11, 1762.
Zaccheus, s. Zach[eu]s and Rebeckah, Feb. 19, 1759.
Zachariah, s. Exp[erience] and Remember, May 14, 1718.
Zachariah, ch. Zachariah and Elizabeth, Aug. 28, 1757.
Zephaniah, s. Zephaniah and Bethiah, June 28, 1715.
Zephaniah, ch. Zephaniah and Hannah, Nov. 19, 1737.
Zephaniah, ch. Zephaniah and Hannah, Feb. 9, 1745.
Zilpa [dup. Zilfa], d. John and Mehitable, Mar. 30, 1718.
―――, d. Ephraim Jr., Apr. 27, 1806.
―――, d. William, Aug. 17, 1806.
―――, d. Seth, Sept. 7, 1806.
―――, d. David, Nov. 6, 1806.
―――, s. Benjamin, [May] 27, 1807.
―――, d. Joseph, July 7, 1807.
―――, d. Abner, [July] 18, 1808.
―――, s. David, [Sept.] 11, 1808.
―――, s. Ephraim, [Sept.] 17, 1808.

26   CHILMARK BIRTHS.

MAYHEW, ———, inf. s. Benjamin and Lydia, Mar. 19, 1809. G.R.
———, d. Smith and Thankful, Aug. 6, 1842.
———, s. Joseph Jr. and Didama, Mar. —, 1844.

McCOLLUM (see MacCollum), Martha, d. Arehable, Apr. 19, 1808.

MITCHELL, Margaret, d. William and Prudence, Mar. 27, 1842. G.R.
Prudence [———], w. William, Apr. 18, 1809. G.R.
William [h. Prudence], Nov. 27, 1805. G.R.

MOSHER, Elihu E., s. James and Harriet Cottle, Nov. 4, 1848.

NICKELSON, Jane, ch. Nathaniel and Lydia, Sept. 3, 1782.
Marany, ch. Nathaniel and Lydia, Oct. 15, 1784.
Mary, ch. Nathaniel and Lydia, Mar. 7, 1781.

NICKERSON, Abigail [w. Benjamin Bassitt], Nov. 22, 1754.
Clarrissa (Hillman) [w. Samuel], Oct. 26, 1805.
Jane, ch. Samuel and Clarrissa, May 23, 1830.
Mary, ch. Samuel and Clarrissa, Sept. 7, 1833.
Samuel [h. Clarrissa (Hillman)], Sept. 2, 1803.
Thomas, ch. Samuel and Clarrissa, Aug. 22, 1835.

NORTON, Almira D., d. Clement and Mary E. (Look), May 2, 1848.
Bethiah, ch. Shobal and Pheobe, Nov. 20, 1758.
Betsey, d. Samuel and Elisabeth, Sept. 10, 1776. [Betsy, G.R.]
Betsey [dup. adds E.], d. William and Martha G., May 13, 1843.
Clement Bassett, ch. William and Polly, Sept. 29, 1794 [sic, see James Will[ia]m].
Clement Bassett, ch. William and Polly, Sept. 10, 1796 [sic, see Elizabeth].
Constant, s. Jacob and Bethia, Dec. 10, 1737.
Desire of Edgartown, July 10, 1731.
Elizabeth, ch. William and Polly, Nov. 26, 1796 [sic, see Clement Bassett].
Eunice (Look) [w. Samuel], Mar. 17, 1791.
Fanny B., d. William and Martha G. (Bassett), June 19, 1847.
Francis, s. Jacob and Bethia, June 6, 1747.
Freman, s. Shobal and Pheobe, Aug. 21, 1754.
Jacob, s. Jacob Jr. and Bethiah, Mar. 5, 1739.
James Will[ia]m, ch. William and Polly, Dec. 18, 1794 [sic, see Clement Bassett].
Love [?], d. Jacob and Bethia, Apr. 7, 1745.

NORTON, Martha G. (Bassett) [w. William], Apr. 7, 1825.
Mary B. [w. Josiah Tillton], Dec. 29, 1792.
Mayhew, s. Jacob and Bethia, Nov. 18, 1749.
Nahum T., s. Aseneth, Aug. 17, 1844.
Peter, s. Jacob and Bethia, Sept. 6, 1742.
Polly Bassett, ch. William and Polly, Dec. 29, 1792.
Rebecah, d. Samuel and Elisabeth, Feb. 8, 1774.
Samuel [h. Eunice (Look)], Sept. 5, 1783 [dup. Sept. 5, 1733].
Sarah, ch. Shobal and Pheobe, May 27, 1756.
Shobal, s. Jacob and Bethia, Aug. 21, 1733.
William, s. Samul and Elisabeth, Oct. 20, 1770.
William, ch. Samuel and Eunice [dup. [h. Martha G. (Bassett)]], Apr. 28, 1812.
William G., ch. William and Martha G., June 26, 1849.
———, s. Thomas of Edgartown, Sept. 15, 1807.
———, [twin] s. Samuel and Eunice, Aug. 3, 1816.
———, [twin] s. Samuel and Eunice, Aug. 3, 1816.

PACKARD, Rebecca H., July 30, 1785. G.R.

PEASE, Sophronia P. [———], w. John Jr., Aug. 12, 1805. G.R.
———, d. Fortunatus Jr., Jan. 10, 1806.
———, s. Nathaniel, Oct. 12, 1807.

POOL (see Poole), ———, s. Ephrim and Martha Jr., Aug. 30, 1842.
———, d. Eph[raim] and Martha, Mar. — [? 1848].

POOLE (see Pool), Anderson T., s. Ephraim and Lucinda Tilton, Oct. 12, 1834.
Elizabeth N., d. Ephraim and Lucinda Tilton, Oct. 27, 1827.
Ephraim, s. Ephraim and Lucinda Tilton, Aug. 3, 1813.
Jane S., d. Ephraim and Lucinda Tilton, July 25, 1815.
Jane S., d. Ephraim and Lucinda Tilton, Mar. 17, 1819.
Jared F., s. Ephraim and Lucinda Tilton, Sept. 27, 1823.
Lavina A., d. Ephraim and Lucinda Tilton, Feb. 17, 1821.
Lucinda, d. Ephraim and Lucinda Tilton, June 13, 1817.
Mary Mayh[e]w, d. Ephraim, July 18, 1806.
Matthew, s. Ephraim and Lucinda Tilton, Aug. 16, 1810.
Parnel T., d. Ephraim and Lucinda Tilton, Apr. 20, 1812.

REED, Frank H., s. Rodney R. and Prudence W. (Cottle), Dec. 28, 1849.
Lemuel B., s. Lemuel and Sophronia Cottle, Dec. 12, 1847.

REED, Rodney R., Sept. 5, 1825. G.R.
Sophronia R., d. Rodney R. and Prudence W. (Cottle), Aug. 30, 1848.

ROBERTSON, Martha, d. John, Aug. 8, 1808.

ROBINSON, Deborah [———], w. Shadrach, Feb. 28, 1761. G.R.
Elisha, ch. Isaac and Mary, Mar. 30, 1763.
Merebah, ch. Isaac and Mary, Jan. 27, 1762.

ROTCH, Francis O., Aug. 14, 1817. G.R.

RUSSELL, Catharine, d. Holder and Deborah, Nov. 29, 1791.

SEARL, Rebeckah, d. Benjamin and Hannah, grand d. Pain Mayhew, Aug. 12, 1754.

SKIFF (see Skiffe), Abigail, d. Joseph and Remember, July 4, 1748.
Anna, ch. James and Ana, Feb. 16, 1753.
Caleb, ch. Joseph and Rem[em]ber, June 18, 1742.
Catharine, ch. Vinal and Catharine, Aug. 8, 1794.
Deborah, ch. James and Ana, Oct. 27, 1749.
Ebenezer, s. Joseph and Remember, Dec. 19, 1750.
Ellis, s. Ebenezer and Deborah, Jan. 28, 1797.
Hannah, d. Nathaniel (Skiffe) and Mary, June 6, 1688.
Hannah, ch. James and Ana, Apr. 15, 1758.
Henry Gorham, s. Stephen D. and Eleanor Davis, May 10, 1846.
James, ch. James and Ana, Feb. 27, 1751.
Joseph, ch. Joseph and Rem[em]ber, Apr. 24, 1745.
Joseph, s. Ebenezer and Deborah, Nov. 1, 1792.
Lidia, d. Stephen and Bethsheba, Nov. —, 1744.
Martha, ch. Stephen and Bathsheba, Feb. 1, 1755.
Martha, ch. Vinal and Catharine, Feb. 19, 1781.
Mercy, ch. Joseph and Rem[em]ber, Apr. 9, 1741.
Nathanil, s. Stephen and Bathsheba, June 16, 1747.
Prince, ch. James and Ana, Dec. 27, 1747.
Rebecca, w. Charles Tilton, Apr. 4, 1820. G.R.
Rebeckah, ch. Stephen and Bathsheba, July 13, 1752.
Rufus, s. Ebenezer and Deborah, May 15, 1794.
Sam[ue]ll, ch. Joseph and Rem[em]ber, Jan. 23, 1743.
Sanders, ch. James and Ana, July 9, 1765.
Stephen, s. Stephen and Bathsheba, June 10, 1750.
Stephen, ch. Vinal and Catharine, Sept. 23, 1787.
Vinal, ch. Stephen and Bathsheba, Feb. 11, 1759.

CHILMARK BIRTHS. 29

SKIFF, Volintine, ch. James and Ana, Aug. 28, 1760.
William E., s. Samuil E. and Eunice M., June 25, 1846.
———, s. Samuel and Eunice, Aug. —, 1849.

SKIFFE (see Skiff), Benjamin, s. Nathan and Hephziba, Apr. 29, 1691.
Elizabeth, d. Nathan and Hephziba, Sept. —, 1690.
James, s. Nathan and Hephziba, Mar. 10, 1689.
James, s. James and Lydia, July 15, 1722.
John, s. Nathan and Mercy, Aug. 22, 1705.
Joseph, s. Nathan and Mercy, Nov. 18, 1709.
Mary, d. Nathan and Hephziba, May 26, 1695.
Mercy, d. Nathan and Mercy, July 5, 1701.
Sam[ue]ll, s. Nathan and Mercy, Dec. 24, 1703.
Sarah, d. Nathan and Mercy, Feb. —, 1698.
Stephen, s. Nathan and Hephziba, May 26, 1693.
Stephen, s. James and Lydia, May 8, 1718.

SLOCUM, Charles, ch. John and Robey, Jan. 9, 1779.
Deborah, ch. John and Robey, Jan. 27, 1776.
Humphery Ames, ch. John and Robey, Sept. 24, 1783.
John Jr., ch. John and Robey, Oct. 6, 1780.
Rodney, ch. John and Robey, Oct. 24, 1785.

SMITH, Abigal, d. Shobal and Martha, Oct. 14, 1724.
Asa, Jan. 21, 1824. G.R.
Austin E., s. Austin E. and Laviner, Feb. 13, 1847.
Benjamin, ch. Elijah and Hannah, May 6, 1769.
Charlotte E., d. Otis and Jane N., Sept. 9, 1846.
Elijah, ch. Elijah and Hannah, June 29, 1771.
Eloisa, d. Rev. Jonathan and Anna, Jan. 13, 1791.
Erastus, s. Rev. Jonathan and Anna, Nov. 1, 1793.
George A., Capt., July 18, 1803. G.R.
Hannah, ch. Elijah and Hannah, Sept. 11, 1777.
Matthew, ch. Elijah and Hannah, May 26, 1786.
Matthew, ch. Elijah and Hannah, Sept. 15, 1787.
Mayhew, ch. Elijah and Hannah, June 26, 1773.
Mayhew, ch. Elijah and Hannah, Oct. 14, 1779.
Otis, s. Mayhew, [Apr.] 27, 1808. [Capt. Otis, G.R.]
Otis E., s. Capt. Otis and Jane N., Nov. 14, 1849. G.R.
Polly, ch. Elijah and Hannah, Nov. 4, 1781.
Rufus, ch. Elijah and Hannah, June 1, 1784.
Sarah, d. Shobal and Martha, Feb. 4, 1728.
Sarah, ch. Elijah and Hannah, May 25, 1775.
———, d. Mayhew, Oct. 1, 1806.

STEAL, John (Steel), ch. John and Mary, Nov. 14, 1721.
Martha, ch. John and Mary, Sept. 21, 1719.

STEWART (see Stuart), Jedidah, Sept. 6, 1758. G.R.
Margaret [w. William Tilton], July 10, 1766.
Prince M., s. George and Jerusha Cottle, Apr. 5, 1846.
Ruhamah, Dec. 29, 1728. G.R.
William, Mar. 20, 1729. G.R.
———, d. William Jr., May 12, 1806.
———, s. George W. and Jerusha, Apr. 20, 1843.

STUART (see Stewart), George W., Oct. 13, 1801. G.R.
Jeremiah, Apr. 24, 1834. G.R.
Jerusha T. (Cottle), w. George W., Oct. 22, 1805. G.R.

SWETT, Jane Ann, w. Edward Mayhew, June 7, 1822. G.R.

TAINTER, Augustus, s. Rev. Nahum and Ann E., June 26, 1846.

TASKER, John, Rev., July 6, 1818, in Ackerington, Eng. G.R.

THOMPSON (see Tompson).

TILLTON (see Tilton), Abiah, ch. William and Bershabe, Feb. 20, 1774.
Abigail, ch. Nathan and Rachal, Mar. 21, 1785.
Albert, ch. Oliver and Eunise, Dec. 5, 1791.
Anna, ch. William and Bershabe, June 30, 1777.
Asa, ch. Reuben and Abigail, Dec. 1, 1769.
Bathsheba, ch. William and Bershabe, Dec. 25, 1769.
Bathsheba, ch. Nathan and Rachal, June 2, 1772.
Beriah, ch. William and Bershabe, June 7, 1763.
Bethiah, ch. Uriah and Jedidah, July 13, 1762.
Charlotte [w. Owen Hillman (Hilliams) Jr.], June 8, 1804. [w. Capt. Owen, G.R.]
Cornelius, ch. Mathew and Sarah, Mar. 25, 1789.
Daniel, ch. Stephen and Rebeckah, Oct. 4, 1771.
Daniel, s. Mathew and Sarah, Feb. 6, 1772.
David, ch. Uriah and Jedidah, May 5, 1752.
Elisha, ch. Uriah and Jedidah, Oct. 23, 1738.
Elisha, ch. Ezra (Tilton) and Mary, Oct. 23, 1782.
Elizabeth Skiff, d. David and Martha, Jan. 24, 1801.
Ezra, ch. Uriah and Jedidah, May 18, 1741.
Frances West, ch. Ezra (Tilton) and Mary, Sept. 9, 1785.

TILLTON, Hannah, ch. Stephen and Rebeckah [dup. [w. John Flanders]], Apr. 4, 1770.
Hannah, ch. William and Bershabe, Oct. 29, 1775.
Hannah, ch. William and Bershabe, Sept. 18, 1783.
Hannah (Flanders) [w. Josiah], Apr. 15, 1799.
Hebron, ch. Mathew and Sarah, Aug. 24, 1787.
Horatio W., ch. Josiah and Mary B., July 21, 1822. [Capt. Horatio W. Tilton, G.R.]
James N., ch. Josiah and Mary B., Jan. 21, 1816. [Tilton [h. Lydia B.], G.R.]
Jedidah, ch. Uriah and Jedidah, Mar. 24, 1755.
Jemima, ch. Reuben and Abigail, July 24, 1764.
Jerusha, ch. Uriah and Jedidah, Nov. 27, 1759.
John, ch. Oliver and Eunise, Aug. 19, 1796.
Jonathan, ch. Uriah and Jedidah, Mar. 1, 1744.
Josiah [h. Mary B. (Norton)], July 16, 1786.
Julinia, ch. Oliver and Eunise, Aug. 8, 1800.
Katharine [Keturah], ch. Ezra (Tilton) and Mary, Aug. 28, 1802.
Lavina, ch. Nathan and Rachal, July 1, 1777.
Lucinda, ch. Mathew and Sarah, Feb. 23, 1791.
Mary, ch. William and Bershabe, Sept. 2, 1764.
Mary B. (Norton) [w. Josiah], Dec. 29, 1792.
Mary B., ch. Josiah and Mary B., Dec. 1, 1819.
Matthew, ch. Mathew and Sarah, Aug. 13, 1779.
Mercy, ch. Uriah and Jedidah, Sept. 5, 1757.
Meribah, ch. Oliver and Eunise, Apr. 12, 1798.
Moses, ch. Nathan and Rachal, July 25, 1782.
Nancy, d. Petter and Sarah, Oct. 9, 1759.
Nathan, ch. Sirano and Remember, May 9, 1736.
Nathan, ch. Nathan and Rachal, Dec. 5, 1779.
Olivia, ch. Mathew and Sarah, Oct. 10, 1777.
Pamelia, ch. Oliver and Eunise, Jan. 3, 1795.
Parnel, ch. Mathew and Sarah, Feb. 18, 1794.
Petter, ch. Thomas and Jemima, July 1, 1733.
Polly, ch. Ezra (Tilton) and Mary, Sept. 24, 1793.
Rachal, ch. Nathan and Rachal, May 2, 1766.
Remember, ch. Nathan and Rachal, Apr. 24, 1769.
Reuben, ch. Thomas and Jemima, Aug. 26, 1735.
Ruth, d. Peter and Sarah, Aug. 27, 1743.
Samuel, ch. Stephen and Rebeckah, Apr. 18, 1773.
Samuel, ch. William and Bershabe, Apr. 14, 1782.
Samuel, ch. Mathew and Sarah, Aug. 18, 1796.
Sarah, ch. Mathew and Sarah, Mar. 14, 1785.

CHILMARK BIRTHS.

TILLTON, Thomas, ch. Reuben and Abigail, Oct. 24, 1766.
Uriah, ch. Uriah and Jedidah, Feb. 11, 1747.
William, June 13, 1734.
William [dup. Tilton], ch. William and Bershabe [dup. [h. Margaret (Stewart)]], Feb. 1, 1767.
Zelinday, ch. Mathew and Sarah, Dec. 24, 1782.
Zephiniah, ch. Uriah and Jedidah, Nov. 2, 1749.

TILTON (see Tillton), Abiah, d. Josiah and Bethshaba, Oct. 27, 1709.
Baze. N., ch. Benjamin S. and Susanna, Mar. 21, 1827.
Benjamin S. [h. Susanna (Hillman)], Mar. 23, 1788. [Mar. 28, G.R.]
Beriah, ch. William and Abiah, Oct. 13, 1703.
Beriah, s. William and Abiah, ———.
Bethsheba, ch. Josiah and Bethsheba, June 22, 1721.
Charles, Dec. 21, 1810. G.R.
C. Laroy, s. Cornelius and Almira, Mar. 11, 1844. G.R.
Cyrano (see Sirano).
David, Sept. 26, 1813. G.R.
Deborah M., ch. William [dup. Jr.] and Margaret, Aug. 25, 1807.
Deborah M., d. Horatio and Thresa, June 27, 1849.
Eliakim, June 14, 1773. G.R.
Elisha, Sept. 23, 1763. G.R.
Eliza Ewins, d. Allen and Mary E. (McCollum), Jan. 19, 1843.
Elizabeth (Tillton), ch. Ezra and Elizabeth, July 26, 1776.
Eunice Foster, d. Alonzo and Corisanda, Dec. 21, 1848.
Fanny [dup. Tillton], ch. William and Margaret [dup. [w. Norton Bassett Jr.]], Aug. 23 [dup. Aug. 22], 1802.
Francis, Dec. 18, 1761. G.R.
Hannah, d. Josiah and Elizabeth, Dec. 23, 1748.
Hepsibah N., July 2, 1784. G.R.
Hugh Cathcart, s. Allen and Mary E. (McCollum), Oct. 26, 1835.
Isadora Brown, d. Allen and Mary E. (McCollum), Feb. 17, 1838.
Jeane, ch. William and Abiah, Aug. 2, 1697.
John, s. John and Sarah, Mar. 24, 1705-6.
Jonathan, June 10, 1770. G.R.
Joseph, s. John and Sarah, Dec. 13, 1710.
Josiah, ch. Josiah and Bethsheba, Aug. 18, 1719.
Lovy, ch. Ezra and Mary, July 26, 1780.
Lucy (Tillton), ch. Ezra and Elizabeth, Feb. 25, 1768.
Margaret (Stewart) [w. William], July 10, 1766.

CHILMARK BIRTHS. 33

TILTON, Margaret, ch. William and Margaret, Apr. 12, 1794.
Martha [name in pencil], ch. Benjamin S. and Susanna, ———
   [? b. after ch. b. Feb. 16, 1836].
Martha J., d. Allen and Mary E. (McCollum), July 9, 1839.
Mary, d. Charles and Rebecca, May ——— [rec. May 25, 1848].
Mercy (Tillton), ch. Ezra and Elizabeth, May 27, 1770.
Owen H., ch. Benjamin S. and Susanna, Feb. 16, 1836.
Pain, s. Josiah and Elizabeth, Sept. 30, 1745.
Prince Allen, s. Allen and Mary E. (McCollum), Apr. 10, 1837.
Rebecca (Skiff), w. Charles, Apr. 4, 1820. G.R.
Ruhamah, ch. William and Margaret, Sept. 22, 1799. [Ruhamah M., G.R.]
Salathiel, s. Josiah and Bathshaba, May 4, 1706.
Samuel, ch. William and Abiah, Feb. 18, 1700.
Samuel M., Oct. 12, 1828. G.R.
Sam[ue]ll, s. John and Sarah, Jan. 17, 1723-4.
Sarah, ch. William and Abiah, Apr. 26, 1701.
Sarah, d. John and Sarah, Aug. 25, 1717.
Sirano, s. John and Sarah, Dec. 10, 1700.
Sophia, ch. William and Margaret, Feb. 12, 1788.
Susanna (Hillman) [w. Benjamin S.], June 7, 1797. [Susan, G.R.]
Theresa, ch. William and Margaret, Apr. 28, 1797.
Thomas, s. John and Sarah, Dec. 4, 1702.
Thomas J., s. Benjamin and Susan, June 7, 1797. G.R.
Thomas J., ch. Benjamin S. and Susanna, May 1, 1829.
Tryphena (Tillton), ch. Ezra and Elizabeth, Nov. 9, 1766.
Uriah, ch. Josiah and Bethsheba, Nov. 15, 1713.
Walter H., ch. Benjamin S. and Susanna, Mar. 15, 1832.
Warren M., Nov. 9, 1798. G.R.
William, ch. William and Margaret, Oct. 28, 1790.
William, s. Beriah and Mary, ———.
William, s. Samuel [and Hannah], ———.
William, s. William and Bathsheba, ———.
Zadoc A., Capt., May 11, 1797. G.R.
Zadock Allen, s. Allen and Mary, May 12, 1845.
———, s. William and Margaret, Apr. 5, 1793.
———, s. Thomas, [Oct.] 27, 1807.
———, ch. Allen and Mary (Tillton), Feb. 25, 1843.

TOMPSON, William, ch. Robert and Jane, Jan. 7, 1769.

VINCENT, Daniel, s. Herman and Louisa, June 30, 1844.
Ellsworth, s. Simon M. [and] Mary O. (Rotch), Dec. 17, 1849.

VINCENT, Elvira D. [———], w. James H., Mar. 10, 1844. G.R.
Herman [h. Louisa], May 6, 1806. G.R.
Jonathan, ch. Ellisha and Mary, May 11, 1728.
Joseph, ch. Ellisha and Mary, May 31, 1731.
Louisa [———], w. Herman, Apr. 27, 1806. G.R.
Margate, ch. Ellisha and Mary, July 9, 1726.
Mary, ch. Ellisha and Mary, Feb. 11, 1727.
Simon M., Mar. 7, 1819. G.R.
———, d. Herman and Louisa, Apr. 7, 1846.

WEEKS, Richard Osbern, s. Arvin L. and Elizabeth, May 14, 1843.

WEST, Ann Maria, d. Leonard and Rebecca, Oct. 19, 1844. [Anna M., Oct. 19, 1845, G.R.]
Daniel W., s. George and Deidama D. (Tilton), Dec. 17, 1849.
David Bates, s. Leonard and Rebecca Flanders, Nov. 6, 1849.
Deidamia D. [———], w. George, July 16, 1818. G.R.
Elizabeth, ch. Leonard and Rebecca, Sept. 16, 1828.
Frances P., d. Moses and Rebecca W., Jan. 30, 1841.
George [h. Deidamia D.], Jan. 27, 1817. G.R.
George, s. George and Deidamia Tilton, Dec. 24, 1847.
Harriet W., d. Moses and Rebecca, Mar. 25, 1848.
Lavina R., d. Moses and Rebecca, July 2, 1846.
Leanard [dup. Leonard], ch. George and Prudence [dup. [h. Rebecca (Flanders)]], Nov. 21, 1797.
Love T., d. Moses and Rebecca W., July 7, 1837.
Lovey, July 7, 1789. G.R.
Lydia, ch. George and Prudence, Nov. 27, 1806.
Lydia [w. Thomas H. Lumbut], ———.
Martha, ch. Leonard and Rebecca, Dec. 16, 1829.
Mary, ch. George and Prudence, May 13, 1800.
Rebecca (Flanders) [w. Leonard], June 29, 1806.
Rebecca S., d. Moses and Rebecca W., Feb. 19, 1839.
Rebecca Tilton, d. George Jr. and Didama, Oct. —, 1844.
Sarah [———], w. Capt. Thomas, Dec. 14, 1755. G.R.
Sarah Elizabeth, d. Moses and Rebecca W., Oct. 28, 1843 [dup. 1844].
Samuel E., s. George and Deidama Tilton, Apr. 24, 1846.
Sophrona, ch. George and Prudence, Apr. 13, 1804.
Thomas, Capt., May 3, 1786. G.R.
———, s. Leonard and Rebecca, Apr. 7, 1843.
———, d. Moses and Rebecca, July —, 1849.

WINPENNY, William, s. William and Hannah, July 22, 1756.

UNIDENTIFIED.

———, Beulah, w. Dea. Ezra Allen, Feb. 26, 1769. G.R.
———, Caroline, w. William Mayhew, Sept. 4, 1800. G.R.
———, Carrissa [w. Norton Bassett], Mar. 23, 1772.
———, Charlotte J., w. John Wesley Mayhew, May 17, 1846. G.R.
———, Deborah, w. Shadrach Robinson, Feb. 28, 1761. G.R.
———, Deborah A. [w. Thomas H. Lumbut], ———.
———, Deidamia D., w. George West, July 16, 1818. G.R.
———, Elvira D., w. James H. Vincent, Mar. 10, 1844. G.R.
———, Fanny, w. Norton Bassett, Aug. 22, 1802. G.R.
———, Jane S., w. Jonathan Mayhew, Mar. 17, 1819. G.R.
———, Louisa, w. Herman Vincent, Apr. 27, 1806. G.R.
———, Lucinda, w. Ephraim Mayhew, June 13, 1817. G.R.
———, Margaret, w. George D. Cottle, Apr. 19, 1800. G.R.
———, Martha G., w. William, Apr. 7, 1825. G.R.
———, Mary A., w. Hiram Hammett, Aug. 26, 1824. G.R.
———, Mary E., w. Oliver, Nov. 16, 1822. G.R.
———, Patince, w. Matthew Allen, Sept. 4, 1777.
———, Prudence, w. William Mitchell, Apr. 18, 1809. G.R.
———, Rebecca [w. Ephrain Allen], Apr. 17, 1782.
———, Sarah, w. Capt. Thomas West, Dec. 14, 1755. G.R.
———, Sarah E., w. George M. Cleveland, ———, 1772. G.R.
———, Sophronia P., w. John Pease Jr., Aug. 12, 1805. G.R.
———, Susan, w. Benjamin S. Tilton, June 7, 1797.
———, Temprance, w. Matthew Allen, Apr. 13, 1780.

CHILMARK MARRIAGES.

CHILMARK MARRIAGES.

To the year 1850.

ADAMS, Abigail and Ebenezer Bassett, May 21, 1780.*
Betsy and Uriel Hillman, Dec. 21, 1797.*
Calvin C., Capt., and Lydia A. Athearn, int. Oct. 10, 1835.
David L. and Phebe Mayhew, int. May 26, 1826.
Love and Shubael Norton, Jan. 11, 1791.*
Lovisa [int. Lovice] and Thomas Norton, Oct. 26, 1806.
Luretia and Henry Robinson, Mar. 15, 1827.
Martha A. [int. Ann] and Matthew Pool, Aug. 27, 1834.
Mayhew and Rebecca Mayhew, Dec. 27, 1750.*
Mayhew and Lydia Russel, Dec. 13, 1792, in Tisbury.*
Mayhew [int. adds Capt.], 32, s. Moses and Martha, and Mary C. Davis, July 20, 1845.
Moses and Martha Look, Mar. 24, 1799, in Tisbury.*
Parnal and Thomas Waid Mayhew, Dec. 21, 1780.*
Rebecca and John Cottle, Dec. 22, 1774.*
Susanna and Sam[ue]l Athearn, [Apr.] 21, 1791.*
Washington and Casandra Hancock, Oct. 10, 1833.
William and Thankful Look, Jan. 14, 1795, in Tisbury.*

ALLEN, Abigal [and] Wilson March, Dec. 9, 1748.*
Bathsheba and John Mills, Oct. 31, 1726.*
Benjamin and Eliza Doane, Sept. —, 1742, in Harwich.*
Betsey and Matthew Coffin, Feb. 21, 1799.*
Betsey A. of Tisbury, and George A. Smith, int. Aug. 19, 1837.
Beulah D. and Elijah Cleavland, int. June 12, 1835.
Catharine of Tisbury, and Sylvanus Allen, Aug. 30, 1792, in Tisbury.*
Desire Jr. and Athearn Butler, Oct. 2, 1788.*
Elizabeth [dup. Elizebeth] and Will[ia]m Waldron, Dec. 28, 1721.*
Elizabeth and Lemuel Lebaron, Dec. 29, 1774.*
Ephraim Jr. and Rebeccah Look, int. Mar. 1, 1807.
Eunice and Dr. Allen Mayhew, Dec. 18, 1795.*

* Intention not recorded.

ALLEN, Ezra and Beulah Coffin, Apr. 6, 1797.*
Hannah and William Laurence, Nov. 5 [1801].
Harriet and Matthew [int. Mathew] Coffin, Apr. 15, 1827.
Henry and Sophia Spaulding, Feb. 19, 1801.
Holder and Mary Slocum, int. Mar. 31, 1832.
Huldah and James Coffin, Sept. 9 [1773].*
Ichabod and Ellizebeth Clifford, Nov. 4, 1728.*
James 3d and Mrs. [dup. omits Mrs.] Lois Allen, Dec. 18, 1783.*
James 3d and Cynthia Cottle, int. Aug. 20, 1803.
Jane and Silas Bassett, Mar. 11, 1779.*
Jane and John Robinson, July 25, 1807.
Jedidah and Abisha Pease, Feb. 28, 1798, in Tisbury.*
John and Margaret Homes, Mar. 1, 1716.*
John and Mary Mayhew, Oct. 17, 1777.*
Jonathan and Abagal Mayhew, Nov. 17, 1733.*
Jonathan and Deborah Gardner, Dec. 31, 1761.*
Joseas [?] and Bersheba Tillton, Nov. 4, 1762.*
Lavinnia of Tisbury, and David Tilton, Oct. 11, 1793, in Tisbury.*
Lois, Mrs. [dup. omits Mrs.], and James Allen 3d, Dec. 18, 1783.*
Mahitable [int. Mehitable], Mrs., of Gayhead, and James Bowyer, June 28, 1847.
Margate and Clemmant Peckam, Oct. 29, 1744.*
Martha and Capt. William Worth, Apr. 5, 1788.*
Mary and Matthew Mayhew, Jan. 3, 1744.*
Mary and Samuel Tillton, May 16, 1768.*
Mary, Mrs., and Shubael Cottle Esq., int. May 26, 1803.
Mary A. and Trueman Cottle, int. Apr. 8, 1837.
Matthew [dup. Mathew] and Patience Allen, Dec. 8, 1796, in Tisbury.*
Matthew and Temperance Allen, Nov. 29, 1798.*
Patience of Tisbry [dup. Tisbury], and Matthew [dup. Mathew] Allen, Dec. 8, 1796, in Tisbury.*
Peggy and Rev. Moses Hallock, Sept. 12, 1792.*
Persis [int. Percy] and George Look, Nov. 27 [1800].
Prudence [int. Jr.] and Will[ia]m B. [int. Brandon] Mayhew, Nov. 6 [1800].
Rebecca and Solomon Butler, ——— [rec. between Sept. 12 and Sept. 20 [?]], 1792.*
Rebecca P. and George W. Dunham, int. Apr. 18, 1840.
Robert and Desire Norton, Dec. 21, 1752 [dup. 1753, *sic*].*
Robert and Mary Tillton Jr. [dup. omits Jr.], Nov. 21, 1793.*

* Intention not recorded.

CHILMARK MARRIAGES. 41

ALLEN, Salathiel and Lucy Norton, Sept. 24, 1783, in Tisbury.*
Samuel Jr. (All[e]n) and Bullah Davis, Feb. 12, 1741, in Falmouth.*
Susanah and Philip Hathaway, July 17, 1765.*
Sylvanus and Catharine Allen, Aug. 30, 1792, in Tisbury.*
Temperance of Tisbury, and Matthew Allen, Nov. 29, 1798.*
Tristram and Clarissa [dup. Clarrissa] Mayhew, Dec. 17, 1795.*
W[illia]m and Sarah Mayhew, Nov. 13, 1737 [dup. 1739, sic].*
William and Love Coffin, Mar. 10, 1779.*
William of New Bedford, and Mehitable Degrass, July 7, 1839.
Zebulon [dup. Sibulon] and Prudence Mayhew, May 7, 1789.*

ALMY, Christopher of Dartmouth, and Elizabeth Sanford, Dec. 30, 1762.*

AMOS, Hepsabah and Francis Peters, int. Dec. 9, 1807.

ASTEN (see Austin), Sarah and Prince Peckham, Nov. 28, 1780.*

ATHEARN, Jethro of Tisbury, and Mary Mayhew, Sept. 8, 1720.*
Lydia A. of Tisbury, and Capt. Calvin C. Adams, int. Oct. 10, 1835.
Mary of Tisbury, and Nathaniel Mayhew, Feb. 20, 1784, in Tisbury.*
Prince D. of Tisbury, and Mary B. Tilton, Nov. 29, 1838.
Sam[ue]l of Tisbury, and Susanna Adams, [Apr.] 21, 1791.*
Zadock A., 21 [int. of Tisbury], and Betsey Flanders, July 5, 1842.

AUSTIN (see Asten), Beriah and Sophronia Robinson, Oct. 1, 1826.*
Edward and Susannah Robinson, Dec. 21, 1778.*

AWKER, Amy P. and Hebron Woormsly, int. Apr. 1, 1809.

BACON, Thomas [dup. Bakon] and Mary Skiff [dup. Skiffe], Sept. 7, 1721.*

BAKER, Abel of New Sharon, and Deborah Mayhew, Aug. 23, 1795.*

BALSTONE (see Baulstone).

BARKER, Hannah, Mrs., of Pembrook, and Jacob Norton, June 8, 1727, in Pembrook.*

* Intention not recorded.

BARTLETT, Jane of Plymouth, and Matthew Claghorn, Oct. 4, 1759, in Plymouth.*

BASSETT, Abigail and Jeremiah Mayhew Jr., Mar. 3, 1768.*
Benjamin [dup. Bassitt] and Abigail Nicholson [dup. Nickerson], Jan. 22, 1778.*
Ebenezer and Abigail Adams, May 21, 1780.*
Elizabeth and Ezra Tillton, Oct. 28 [? 23], 1765.*
Elizabeth and Zadock Davis, Nov. 15, 1804.
Fortunatus and Sarah Bassett, Feb. 9, 1769.*
John and Jean Mayhew, July 31, 1735.*
John and Ann Hillman, Mar. 7, 1776.*
Martha and Nathan Bassett, Mar. 17, 1776.*
Martha G. and William Norton, June 30, 1842.
Mary and Nathan Bassett, June 9, 1763.*
Nathan and Mary Bassett, June 9, 1763.*
Nathan and Martha Bassett, Mar. 17, 1776.*
Nathan and Lydia Norton, Sept. 22, 1791.*
Nathan and Priscilla Mayhew, Oct. 29, 1828.
Nathan S. and Deborah M. Tilton, Nov. 8, 1827.
Nathaniel [dup. Esq.], s. William and Anna, and Katharine [dup. Katherine] Boardman, May 2 [dup. May 1], 1788.*
Norton and Charissa [dup. Carrissa] Stewart, [Sept.] 22 [dup. Sept. 12], 1791.*
Norton Jr. and Fanny Tillton, Apr. 10, 1823.*
Polly and W[illia]m Norton, Nov. 10, 1791.*
Sarah and Fortunatus Bassett, Feb. 9, 1769.*
Silas and Jane Allen, Mar. 11, 1779.*
Susanna and Hilyard Mayhew, Feb. 16, 1764.*
Theresa [int. Thresa] T., 18, d. Nathan S. and Deborah, and Horatio W. Tilton, Apr. 15, 1847.
William and Olivia Tillton, Nov. 16, 1794.*

BATES, Abiah of Gayhead, and Lewis Cook, July 19, 1838.

BAULSTONE, Hannah, Mrs., of Boston, and Capt. Mayhew Cottle, int. Mar. 2, 1839.

BELANE, George of Chapaquidic, and Sophia Peters, int. Oct. 16, 1835.

BESSE (see Bessey), Lot of Fairhaven, and Hannah G. Tillton, int. Nov. 23, 1833.

BESSEY (see Besse), Willard, 25, s. Lothrop and Malintha, and Mary E. [int. C.] Lake, Feb. 1, 1846.

* Intention not recorded.

CHILMARK MARRIAGES.   43

BLACKWELL, Mary of Sandwich, and Frederick Mayhew, int. Jan. 15, 1836.
Samuel, Capt. [int. omits Capt.], of Nantucket, and [int. adds Mrs.] Martha Mayhew, Aug. —, 1833.

BOARDMAN (see Bordman), Katharine [dup. Katherine] and Nathaniel Bassett [dup. Esq.], May 2 [dup. May 1], 1788.*
Walter and Jane Hillman, Dec. 4, 1790.*

BORDMAN (see Boardman), Abigail and Nathan Mayhew, Nov. 8, 1781.*
[? Bordman], Cathrine, Mrs. (Bordnn), and Shubal Cottle Esq., Nov. 23, 1780.*

BOURNE, Remember of Sandwich, and Experience Mayhew, Dec. 4, 1711.*

BOWYER, James of Gayhead, and Mrs. Mahitable [int. Mehitable] Allen, June 28, 1847.

BRADFORD, Sam[ue]l and Lydia Pease, Nov. 25, 1762.*

BRIGGS, Ephraim of Westport, and Mrs. Parnal Tillton, Sept. 6, 1832.

BROOKS, William [int. Williams] L. of Gayhead, and Mary Manning, July 26, 1839.

BROWN, Thomas of Henniker, N.H., and Mary Smith, Apr. 1, 1832.

BRUCH, Philip of Conn., and Mrs. Hannah Gardner, int. Oct. 3, 1846.

BURGES (see Burgis), Benj[ami]n and Abigail Peas, Feb. 25, 1740.*
Mary and Will[ia]m Poole, Dec. 10, 1767.*

BURGIS (see Burges), Jonathan and Meribah Tillton, Jan. 27, 1785.*

BURRIG, Peleg and Mary Mayhew, Sept. 20, 1742.*

BUTLER, Athearn and Desire Allen Jr., Oct. 2, 1788.*
Dan[ie]ll and Keziah Mayhew, Oct. 8, 1730.*
David and Ann Hach, Dec. 4, 1725.*
Fenious and Cloe Hammon, May 17, 1781.*
Jemima of Tisbury, and Isaac Tilton, Nov. 25, 1790, in Tisbury.*

* Intention not recorded.

CHILMARK MARRIAGES.

BUTLER, Jeremiah and Hannah Robinson, Nov. 14, 1781.*
Mary and Will[ia]m Worth, Oct. 24, 1717.*
Matthew [int. Mathew] P. of Edgartown, and Martha Roberson [int. Baberson], Oct. 29, 1835.
Nicholas [dup. Nicholos] and Lucy Norton, Nov. 5, 1789.*
Phineus and Hannah Robinson, Mar. 3, 1743.*
Prudence and Shadrach Hillman, Mar. 20, 1794.*
Rhoda and Moses Nye, Nov. 11, 1793.*
Sarah and Thomas West, Dec. 21, 1775.*
Solomon and Rebecca Allen, ——— [rec. between Sept. 12 and Sept. 20 [?]], 1792.*
Thomas of Edgartown, and Katharine Stewart, Apr. 5, 1776.*
Timothy of Edgartown, and Jedidah Tillton, Dec. 21, 1780.*

CARTURIGHT (see Cartwright), Edward and Jean Megee, Jan. 1, 1749.*

CARTWRIGHT (see Carturight), Bryant and Elizabeth Weeks, Oct. 19, 1732.*

CATHCART, Robert and Mary Jons, Dec. 11, 1755.*

CHACE (see Chase), Mary [dup. Chase] and Richard Crookes, July 9 [dup. June 7], 1720.*

CHAMBERLIN, W. and Anna H. Robinson, Sept. 25, 1825.*

CHASE (see Chace), Abil and Mercy Mayhew, Feb. 14, 1744.*
Elizabeth of Tisbury, and Ward Tilton, Nov. 3, 1784, in Tisbury.*
Joseph of Tisbury, and Martha Hillman, Nov. 26, 1772.*
Lydia [dup. Chace] and Moses Hillman, Sept. 11, 1794.*
Olive of Tisbury, and James Norton Jr., Mar. 26, 1783, in Tisbury.*
Patience G., 16, of Tisbury, and Rufus N. Smith, Aug. —, 1843.
Sarah and Thomas Cocks, Nov. 12, 1786.*
Zepheniah and Abigail Skiffe, Oct. 10, 1773.*

CHENEY, Lydia and Oliver Slocum, Sept. 7, 1792.*

CHIPMAN, Martha of Barnstable, and Freeman Norten, Apr. 19, 1774.*
Mercy of Barnstable, and Nathan Skiff, Dec. 13, 1699, in Sandwich.*

CHURCH, Caleb and Mercy Pope, Jan. 29, 1752.*
Deborah and Ichabod Stodard, Aug. 9, 1749.*

* Intention not recorded.

CHURCHILL, W[illia]m 3d of Plympton, and Peggy Tillton, —— [rec. between Apr. 14 and Apr. 21], 1791.*

CLAGHERN (see Claghorn), Dorcus and Shubal Pease, Nov. 5, 1761.*

CLAGHORN (see Claghern), James and Salome Cottle, Feb. 17, 1774.*
Matthew and Jane Bartlett, Oct. 4, 1759, in Plymouth.*
Shobal and Martha Hilman, Jan. 7, 1748.*

CLARK (see Clerk), Bethiah and Sam[ue]ll Coos, Feb. 14, 1743.*
Hannah and William Wimpenney, Feb. 26, 1746.*
Mary and Isaac Cottle, Aug. 24, 1749.*

CLEAVLAND, Elijah of Tisbury, and Beulah D. Allen, int. June 12, 1835.
George W. [int. Cleveland] of Tisbury, and Aurilla [int. Aurelia A.] Hancock, Oct. 12, 1831.

CLERK (see Clark), William of Plymouth, and Bethiah Mayhew, Sept. 4, 1707.*

CLIFFORD, Ellizebeth and Ichabod Allen, Nov. 4, 1728.*
Jacob and Bathsheba Skiff, Nov. 8, 1742.*
John of Tisbury, and Almira Look, Aug. 14, 1827.
Mary and Sam[ue]ll Hach, Dec. 1, 1724.*
Ruth (Cliffor[d]) of Tisbury, and Elishai Tillton, int. Feb. 22, 1804.
Sarah and David Donham, Apr. 11, 1723.*
Thomas of Tisbury, and Asenath P. [int. W. [?]] Mayhew, July 23, 1836.

COCKRAN, William and Expereance Weeks, Nov. 1, 1758, in Falmouth.*

COCKS (see Cox), Thomas and Sarah Chase, Nov. 12, 1786.*

COFFIN, Beulah and Ezra Allen, Apr. 6, 1797.*
Hephsabah of Edgartown, and Abisha Haden Lumber[t], Oct. 16, 1792.*
James of Edgartown, and Huldah Allen, Sept. 9 [1773].*
Love and William Allen, Mar. 10, 1779.*
Matthew of Edgartown, and Betsey Allen, Feb. 21, 1799.*
Matthew [int. Mathew] and Harriet Allen, Apr. 15, 1827.

* Intention not recorded.

COLE, Ann and Joshua Johnson, int. Nov. 27, 1808.
John and Anny Horsewit, int. June 10, 1804.

COOK, Almira of Gayhead, and Abel Manning, May 24, 1844.
Austina [Fostenia, written above] of Gayhead, and Thomas Francis, int. Mar. 2, 1836.
Elizabeth of Gayhead, and Alexander Cuff, int. Apr. 21, 1838.
Elizabeth [int. Elisabeth] of Gayhead, and Almoth Howwaswee, June 4, 1840.
Lewis of Gayhead, and Abiah Bates, July 19, 1838.
Mary of Gayhead, and Philip Johnson, int. May 2, 1840.
Thaddeus of Gayhead, and Anna Cooper, int. Oct. 7, 1840.
Thaddeus of Gay Head, and Emily Sailsbury, int. Oct. 4, 1849.
Thadeus of Edgartown, and Polly Johnson, int. Oct. 19, 1805.

COOPER, Aaron Jr. of Gayhead, and Lucy Peters, int. May 30, 1840.
Anna of Gayhead, and Thaddeus Cook, int. Oct. 7, 1840.
Anna, Mrs., of Gayhead, and David T. [int. Daniel F.] Nevers, Jan. 1, 1843.
Bethiah and Amos Jeffers, int. Jan. 15, 1806.
Cindrilla of Gayhead, and James W. Degrass, int. Nov. 17, 1838.
Clarissa of Gayhead, and William Shepherd, int. May 21, 1841.
Coombs of Gayhead, and Anna Hawwossuee, int. July 6, 1835.
James and Elizabeth Johnson, int. Feb. 13, 1805.
Louisa of Gayhead, and Thomas Corvet, int. Apr. 15, 1836.
Louisa of Gayhead, and George David, int. Sept. 27, 1836.
Lovina and George David, int. Mar. 9, 1827.
Mary and William Ephraems, int. July 24, 1802.
Nathan F. and Abiah Maning, int. May 27, 1837.
Prudence of Gayhead, and Samuel Hannet, int. July 10, 1827.
Thomas Jr. and Susannah Tockquenett [Indians], Dec. 13, 1798.*
Thomas [int. of Gayhead] and Mrs. Jane Wormsley, May 7, 1837.

COOS, Sam[ue]ll of Glocester, Essex Co., and Bethiah Clark, Feb. 14, 1743.*

CORVET, Thomas of New Bedford, and Louisa Cooper, int. Apr. 15, 1836.

* Intention not recorded.

CHILMARK MARRIAGES. 47

COTTE (see Cottel, Cottle), Thankful V. [? Cottle] and Smith Mayhew, int. Feb. 3, 1827.

COTTEL (see Cotte, Cottle), Lydia and John Stuart, Dec. 24, 1772.*
Relian[c]e and Lemel Lumb[e]r[t], Oct. 14, 1756.*

COTTEN, Miles and Mary Hix, July 27, 1721.*

COTTLE (see Cotte, Cottel), Abishai and Catharine ———, Nov. 3, 1765.*
Almira D., 16, b. Tisbury, d. George and Margaret, and Augustus Holmes, Mar. 21, 1847.
Amy of Tisbury, and Constant Norton, Sept. 11, 1788, in Tisbury.*
Caroline and James Mayhew, int. June 27, 1835.
Cynthia and James Alien, int. Aug. 20, 1803.
Davis of Tisbury, and Abigail Mayhew, int. Apr. 8, 1837.
Elizabeth [int. Betcy] and Seth Mayhew, June 4 [1801].
Emily A., 23, d. Mayhew and Sarah, and James L. Merry, Oct. 7 [? 11], 1846.
Irenea W. [int. Irena, omits W.], 33, d. Mayhew and Sarah, and James Look, Oct. 6, 1846.
Isaac and Mary Clark, Aug. 24, 1749.*
Jane M., 19, d. George and Margaret, and Alfred Look, July 20, 1845.
Jerusha T. and George W. Stewart, Sept. 15, 1831.
John and Mary West, Dec. 3, 1717.*
John and Zerviah Hillman, Jan. 6, 1731.*
John and Rebecca Adams, Dec. 22, 1774.*
John Jr. and Caroline Williams, int. Mar. 5, 1809.
John, s. Mayhew and Sally, and Margaret W. Sprague, Nov. 23, 1847 [int. 1877, *sic*].
Judeth and James Hatch, Mar. 22, 1719–20.*
Lot of Tisbury, and Catharine [int. Katharine] Smith, Sept. 30, 1804.
Lydia and Joseph Hach, Dec. 30, 1726.*
Mary of Tisbury, and Rhodolphus Hancock, int. Aug. 31, 1827.
Mayhew and Sary Tilton Jr. [int. Tillton, omits Jr.], Dec. 13, 1804.
Mayhew, Capt., and Mrs. Hannah Baulstone, int. Mar. 2, 1839.
Prudence, 17, d. Francis and Sophronia, and Rodney R. Reed, Nov. 6, 1846.
Sally D. and John Hammett, Dec. 20, 1825.*

* Intention not recorded.

COTTLE, Salome and James Claghorn, Feb. 17, 1774.*
Sam[ue]ll and Abigal Mery, Oct. 23, 1724.*
Sarah and Mayhew Smith, int. Mar. 12, 1803.
Selvanus and Martha Hach, Dec. 9, 1725.*
Shubael Esq. of Tisbury, and Mrs. Mary Allen, int. May 26, 1803.
Shubal Esq. of Tisbury, and Mrs. Cathrine Bordnn [? Bordman], Nov. 23, 1780.*
Silas and Jerusha Tillton, Nov. 27, 1777.*
Silas and Jemima Tillton, Mar. 19, 1795.*
Silvanus (C[o]ttle) and Abigail Sherman, Feb. 18, 1745.*
Sophronia W., 19, d. Francis and Sophronia, and Lemuel B. [int. R.] Reed, Nov. 6, 1846.
Trueman and Mary A. Allen, int. Apr. 8, 1837.
William and Anna [int. Anny] B. Williams, Jan. 23, 1806.

COTTON (see Cotten).

COX (see Cocks), Sarah, Mrs., and Capt. Samuel Manter, int. Nov. 14, 1801.

CROOKES, Richard and Mary Chace [dup. Chase], July 9 [dup. June 7], 1720.*

CROWELL, Jonathan of Tisbury, and Remember Tillton, Apr. 14, 1791.*
William H. [int. Crowel], 26, b. Tisbury, of Tisbury, s. Jeremiah and Olive of Tisbury, and Mary M. Sprague, July 21, 1846.

CUFF (see Cuffe), Alexander of Gayhead, and Elizabeth Cook, int. Apr. 21, 1838.
Cloe and Paul Wainier, int. Sept. 29, 1804.
John and Chloe Dodge, int. Aug. 5, 1800.
Jonathan of Gayhead, and Hannah Peters, Apr. 12, 1843.
Lydia and Samuel Johnson, int. Nov. 20, 1808.

CUFFE (see Cuff), Hannah of Gayhead, and Samuel Mingoe, Aug. 21, 1831.

DAGGETT, Isaac of Tisbury, and Abigail Robinson, int. Dec. 15, 1838.
Martha L. of Falmouth, and William F. Sprague, int. Aug. 13, 1847.
Michal of Tisbury, and Remember Nye, int. Mar. 3, 1804.

* Intention not recorded.

CHILMARK MARRIAGES.

DAVID, George of Gayhead, and Lovina Cooper, int. Mar. 9, 1827.
George of Gayhead, and Louisa Cooper, int. Sept. 27, 1836.
James and Peggy Horswet [Indians], int. Apr. 13, 1805.
Lyddia and Nathan Francis, int. Mar. 16, 1811.

DAVIS, Bullah of Falmouth, and Samuel All[e]n Jr., Feb. 12, 1741, in Falmouth.*
David of Edgartown, and Olive Mayhew, Nov. 30, 1786.*
Deidamia and Joseph Tillton Jr., Dec. 25, 1788.*
Hannah of Falmouth, and Zephanieh Robinson Jr., July 29, 1787, in Falmouth.*
John and Mrs. Mary Ann Printice, Apr. 13, 1843.
Levi of Kennebeck, and Lucinda Mayhew, int. Mar. 2, 1827.
Mary C., 19, d. John and Sophronia, and [int. adds Capt.] Mayhew Adams, July 20, 1845.
Rufus of Edgartown, and Rebecca Mayhew, Dec. 4, 1794.*
Rufus H. of Edgartown, and Abigail Hillman, int. Sept. 26, 1840.
Shubel of Edgartown, and Matilda S. Johnson, int. Mar. 19, 1836.
Zadock of Edgartown, and Elizabeth Bassett, Nov. 15, 1804.

DEANE (see Doane), John [? Doane] of Lebanon, Conn., and Ladia Thacher, June 10, ——.*

DE GRASS (see Degrass), Recol [int. Recall] and Abiah Paul [int. [Indians]], Feb. 13, 1805.

DEGRASS (see De Grass), James W. of Tisbury, and Cindrilla Cooper, int. Nov. 17, 1838.
Mehitable of Gayhead, and William Allen, July 7, 1839.

DE VINE (see Divine), John of New Bedford, and Hannah Johnson, int. July 4, 1801.

DEXTER, Allen, Capt., of Rochester, and Martha Mayhew, int. Mar. 2, 1827.
Deberah of Rotchester, and Samuel Hilton, Apr. 23, 1719.*

DIVINE (see De Vine), John of Gayhead, and Parnel Jeffers, int. May 2, 1834.

DOANE (see Deane), Eliza of Harwich, and Benjamin Allen, Sept. —, 1742, in Harwich.*

* Intention not recorded.

DODGE, Chloe and John Cuff, int. Aug. 5, 1800.
Margaret and Calo Pond, int. Aug. 28, 1807.
Mary and Nathaniel Peters, int. Oct. 12, 1806.

DONHAM (see Dunham), David and Sarah Clifford, Apr. 11, 1723.*

DORRIGE (see Porrige).

DUNHAM (see Donham), Abigail N. of Tisbury, and Davis A. Look, int. Nov. 9, 1826.
Charles F. of Edgartown, and Matilda V. Mayhew, int. June 6, 1840.
Dan[ie]ll and Sarah Huxford, Nov. 19, 1739.*
Eleazer of Tisbur[y], and Dinah Tillton, int. Oct. 4, 1800.
George W. of Tisbury, and Rebecca P. Allen, int. Apr. 18, 1840.
John of Tisbury, and Nancy S. Mayhew, Aug. 6, 1839.
Jese of Edgartown, and Dinah Tillton, Mar. 23, 1769.*
Jethro of Edgartown, and Lyda Tillton, Apr. 10, 1776.*
Polly and Matthew Tilton, Apr. 1, 1806.
Thankfull and Timothy Stuart, ——, 1763.*

DURFEE, Allen W. and Phebe Ann [int. Anne] Robinson, —— [int. Sept. 24], 1831.

ELLIS, Deborah of Plymouth, and Ebenezar Skiff, Dec. 29, 1791, in Plymouth.*

EPHRAEMS (see Ephraim), William of Plymouth, and Mary Cooper, int. July 24, 1802.

EPHRAIM (see Ephraems), Molly and Johnson Peters, int. Nov. 4, 1807.

FERGUSON, Helen [int. Hellen] M., 19, of Tisbury, d. John and Sarah, and [dup. and int. add Capt.] Shadrack [dup. Shaduck, int. Shadrach] R. Tilton, Nov. 4, 1847.
William and Deborah Luce, Dec. 11, 1793, in Tisbury.*

FIFIELD, George of Edgartown, and Catharine S. Norton, int. Feb. 26, 1842.

FISHER, Richard of Edgartown, and Lydia West, Nov. 9, 1799.*

FLANDERS, Betsey and Cyrus Hatch, Sept. 1, 1791.*
Betsey, 19, and Zadock A. Athearn, July 5, 1842.
Daniel and Charlotte Smith, Jan. 24, 1830.

* Intention not recorded.

FLANDERS, Daniel, Capt. [int. 41], and Mrs. Jane Manter, Mar. 5, 1843.
Hannah Jr. [dup. omits Jr.] and Josiah Tilton [dup. Tillton], Oct. 21, 1829.
John and Sarah Hillman, Jan. 27, 1769.*
John Jr. [dup. omits Jr.] and Hannah Tillton, Dec. 23, 1792.*
Rebecca and Leonard West, May 5, 1826.*
Richard, Capt., and Parnal Pool, June 6, 1832.
Samuel and Keziah [dup. and int. Kaziah] F. Lumbert, Apr. 2, 1837.
William, Capt., and Agnes L. Tilton, int. Jan. 25, 1840.

FOLGER, Abishai and Sarah Mayhew, Nov. 6, 1727.*

FRANCIES (see Francis), Jane of Gayhead, and Hebron Wamsley, int. Aug. 14, 1846.

FRANCIS (see Francies), Molly and Matthew Gersham, int. Nov. 14, 1807.
Nathan Jr. [dup. omits Jr.] and Esther Rogers, Feb. 26, 1795.*
Nathan and Lyddia David, int. Mar. 16, 1811.
Thomas and Betcy Spaniard, int. May 23, 1800.
Thomas of Gayhead, and Alice Quapish, int. Aug. 11, 1827.
Thomas of Gayhead, and Austina [Fostenia, written above] Cook, int. Mar. 2, 1836.

FRAYNE, Walter, 44, b. New Bedford, of New Bedford, s. Walter and Ann, and Elizabeth R. [dup. N.] Hammett, Nov. 28, 1847.

FULLER, Joseph and Martha Hathaway, June 13, 1717, in Falmouth.*

GARDNER, Deborah and Jonathan Allen, Dec. 31, 1761.*
George W. of Newport, R.I., and Mrs. Hannah Manning, int. Feb. 24, 1838.
Hannah, Mrs., of Gayhead, and Philip Bruch, int. Oct. 3, 1846.

GERSHAM (see Gershom), Matthew and Molly Francis, int. Nov. 14, 1807.

GERSHOM (see Gersham), Joseph and Peggy Tockquenett Jr. [Indians], Aug. 22, 1796.*

GIBS, Remember and Joseph Skiff, July 7, 1740.*
Sarah and John Tilton, Aug. 30, 1738.*

* Intention not recorded.

CHILMARK MARRIAGES.

GIFFERD (see Gifford), Rose and Fortunatus Pease, Nov. 28, 1788.*

GIFFORD (see Gifferd), Daniel P. and Mary Robinson, Nov. 18, 1830.
Eliza and Thomas P. [int. omits P.] Mann, Apr. 6, 1831.
Eliza A. and Simeon F. Hamlin, int. Apr. 14, 1832.
Elizabeth and Nathaniel Pease, Feb. 21, 1796.*
Fear and Cornelius Robinson, Apr. 21, 1792.*
Hulda [int. Huldah] R., 19, d. Amassa and Lydia, and James Winslow, Nov. 14, 1844.
Huldah of Falmouth, and Elihu Robinson, Sept. 8, 1779, in Falmouth.*
John W. and Hannah B. Weeks, int. Nov. 24, 1840.
Nancy A. and Abraham [int. adds C.] White, Sept. 11, 1833.
Polly and Stephen Robinson, June 22, 1796.*
Silas and Ruth Peabody, Mar. 23, 1788.*

GODFREY, Patty and Archabald McCollum, Apr. 24 [1800].*

GOFF, William [int. 32], s. William [and] Sarah, and Lydia S. [int. Susen] Tilton, Dec. 17, 1843.

GOODWIN, Sarah, Mrs., of Gayhead, and Charles Mingo, int. May 6, 1837.

GRAY, Freeman of Tisbury, and Betsey Nichols, Oct. 11, 1798.*
Hannah of Tisbury, and John Mayhew Jr., Jan. 15, 1783, in Tisbury.*
John [of] Tisbyry, and Mary Tillton, Feb. 17, 1789.*

GREEN, Abigal and Jeremiah Robinson, —— 9, 1757.*

GREGREY, Elizabeth and Wadsworth Mayhew, Oct. 5, 1775.*

HACH (see Hatch), Ann and David Butler, Dec. 4, 1725.*
Ichobud of Falmoth, and Elizabeth Tufs, May 18, 1781.*
Joseph and Lydia Cottle, Dec. 30, 1726.*
Martha and Selvanus Cottle, Dec. 9, 1725.*
Sam[ue]ll and Mary Clifford, Dec. 1, 1724.*

HALLOCK, Moses, Rev., of Plainfield, and Peggy Allen, Sept. 12, 1792.*

HAMLIN, Simeon F. of Falmouth, and Eliza A. Gifford, int. Apr. 14, 1832.

* Intention not recorded.

CHILMARK MARRIAGES. 53

HAMMETT (see Hannet), Benj[amin] of Tisbury, and Mrs. Olive Hillman, Dec. 1, 1791.*
Elizabeth R., 51 [dup. Elizabeth N., 41], b. Tisbury, d. Abijah and Olivia, and Walter Frayne, Nov. 28, 1847.
Hiram, 25, b. Tisbury, s. Franklin and B., and Mary A. Tilton, Sept. 28, 1845.
John of Tisbury, and Sally D. Cottle, Dec. 20, 1825.*
Jon[a]th[a]n and Mary Hilman, Oct. 25, 1744.*

HAMMON, Cloe and Fenious Butler, May 17, 1781.*

HANCOCK, Aurilla [int. Aurelia A.] and George W. Cleavland [int. Cleveland], Oct. 12, 1831.
Betsey W. and William M. Lumbert, Oct. 30, 1828.
Casandra and Washington Adams, Oct. 10, 1833.
Cyrus, 39, s. Samuel and Frances, and Thankful Mantor, Dec. 26, 1844.
Deborah R. and Ephraim Harding, int. Aug. 26, 1835.
Mary, Mrs., and Thomas T. Mayhew, int. May 3, 1845.
Rhodolphus and Mary Cottle, int. Aug. 31, 1827.

HANNET (see Hammett), Samuel of Christiantown, and Prudence Cooper, int. July 10, 1827.

HARDING, Ephraim of Tisbury, and Deborah R. Hancock, int. Aug. 26, 1835.

HARISON, Charls and Mercy Porrige [? Dorrige], Feb. 20, 1800.*

HASKINS (see Hoskins).

HATCH (see Hach), Abiah and Isaac Parker, Sept. 10, 1773.*
Anna of Falmouth, and Zepheniah Robenson, Feb. 27, 1757, in Falmouth.*
Benj[ami]n and Reliance Mayhew, Jan. 14, 1762.*
Cyrus and Betsey Flanders, Sept. 1, 1791.*
Ichabod of Falmouth, and Abegail Weeks, Sept. 2, 1714, in Falmouth.*
James and Judeth Cottle, Mar. 22, 1719–20.*
Nathan of Falmouth, and Mary Weeks, Sept. 2, 1714, in Falmouth.*
Reuben and Lucy Tillton, Dec. 3, 1789.*

HATHAWAY, Martha of Falmouth, and Joseph Fuller, June 13, 1717, in Falmouth.*
Philip of Dartmouth, and Susanah Allen, July 17, 1765.*

* Intention not recorded.

HAWKS, Fear and Thomas Tilton, May 11, 1805.
Keziah and Waren Lewis, int. May 8, 1802.
Sylvia and Benj[amin] Richardson, Mar. 24, 1791.*

HAWWOSSUEE (see Hourvoiwee, Howwaswee), Anna of Gayhead, and Coombs Cooper, int. July 6, 1835.

HAYDEN, Mary D., 26, d. John and Lucretia, and Holder R. Tripp, Jan. 1, 1846.

HAZZARD, Eliza and Prince Johnson, int. May 8, 1835.

HENERY (see Henry), Joseph of R.I., and Mrs. Sarah Paull, int. Aug. 2, 1802.

HENRY (see Henery), Sarah, Mrs., of Gayhead, and Philip Johnson, int. Sept. 12, 1845.

HERENDEEN, Sanford and Temperance S. [int. Patience] Robinson, N[ov.] 18, 1827.

HICKS (see Hix).

HILLMAN (see Hilman), Abigail and Rufus H. Davis, int. Sept. 26, 1840.
Ann and John Bassett, Mar. 7, 1776.*
Bathsheba and Francis N. Luce, Nov. 15, 1831.
Celina and Capt. Edwin A. Luce, July 16, 1837.
Clarissa [dup. Clarrissa] and Samuel Nickerson, May 17, 1829.
Deborah and Lot Norton, Dec. 4, 1777.*
Edward and Lydia Hillman, Dec. 9, 1787.*
Eliza and Ira F. Luce, Mar. 1, 1836.
Eliza[be]th and Japhet Turner, Apr. 21, 1763.*
Enice and Robert Look, May 30, 1779.*
Fear and Jeremiah Mayhew, Apr. 7, 1776.*
Hannah and John Peas, Feb. 22, 1776.*
Harriet N., 17, d. Jireh and Nancy, and Moses C. Vincent, Mar. 20, 1846.
Henry and Sorah Mayhew, [Dec.] 9, 1790.*
Isaiah and Sarah Lumbert, int. Jan. 3, 1846.
Jane and Walter Boardman, Dec. 4, 1790.*
Jain [int. Jane] N. and Otis Smith, Oct. 30, 1833.
Lois and Daniel Look, Oct. 7, 1804.
Lot and Lovey Luce, June 20, 1780, in Tisbury.*
Love of New Bedford, and Robert Hillman Jr., int. Nov. 9, 1807.

* Intention not recorded.

CHILMARK MARRIAGES.

HILLMAN, Lydia and Nathaniel Nicholson, Sept. 21, 1780.*
Lydia and Edward Hillman, Dec. 9, 1787.*
Martha and Joseph Chase, Nov. 26, 1772.*
Mary N. [int. omits N.] and Shubal Norton, Feb. 21, 1828.
Moses and Lydia Chase [dup. Chace], Sept. 11, 1794.*
Nancy and Prince Hillman, July 18 [1801].*
Nancy, Mrs., and Samuel Look Jr., int. Mar. 6, 1808.
Olive, Mrs., and Benj[amin] Hammett, Dec. 1, 1791.*
Owen and Polly Norton, Aug. 20, 1795.*
Owen Jr. (Hillmar) [dup. Hilliams] and Charlotte Tilton [dup. and int. Tillton], June 16 [dup. June 17], 1828.
Parnell and Thomas Lumbert, Oct. 30, 1791.*
Prince and Nancy Hillman, July 18 [1801].*
Prudence and Abraham [int. Abram] Knowles, July 9, 1807.
Rebeca and Robert Hillman, May 11, 1769.*
Richard and Jone Thompson, July 3, 1775.*
Robert and Rebeca Hillman, May 11, 1769.*
Robert Jr. and Love Hillman, int. Nov. 9, 1807.
Ruth and Thomas Thorp, Mar. 17, 1768.*
Sarah and John Flanders, Jan. 27, 1769.*
Shadrach and Prudence Butler, Mar. 20, 1794.*
Silas Jr. and Sukey Jones, Nov. 21, 1798.*
Silas and Mary B. Norton, Oct. 29, 1835.
Stephen and Bathsheba [int. Bersheba] Skiff, Apr. 24, 1806.
Susanah and Benj[amin] Skiff Jr., Dec. 12, 1765.*
Susanna and Benjamin S. Tilton, Oct. 24, 1822.*
Uriel and Betsy Adams, Dec. 21, 1797.*
Whitten and Olive Roch, Sept. 2, 1784, in Tisbury.*
Zerviah and John Cottle, Jan. 6, 1731.*

HILMAN (see Hillman), Ezra and Zerviah Jones, Dec. 4, 1766.*
Jean and Eben[e]z[e]r Jones, Sept. 21, 1733.*
Jonathan and Keziah Luce, June 29, 1749.*
Martha and Shobal Claghorn, Jan. 7, 1748.*
Mary and Jon[a]th[a]n Hammett, Oct. 25, 1744.*
Mehetabel and John Merry, ———.*
Rhoda and Malachi Merry, June 26, 1766.*
Silas and Susanah Mayhew, Dec. 4, 1755.*

HILTON, Samuel and Deberah Dexter, Apr. 23, 1719.*

HIX, Mary and Miles Cotten, July 27, 1721.*

* Intention not recorded.

HOLISTER, Abigail of Edgartown, and Daniel Luce, int. Sept. 16, 1803.

HOLMES (see Homes), Augustus, 26, b. Hanover, N.H. [int. of Hanover, N.H.], s. Robert and Rebecca of Hanover, N.H., and Almira D. Cottle, Mar. 21, 1847.

HOMES (see Holmes), Margaret and John Allen, Mar. 1, 1716.*

HORSEWIT (see Horswet), Anny and John Cole, int. June 10, 1804.

HORSWET (see Horsewit), Peggy and James David [Indians], int. Apr. 13, 1805.

HORTON, Lydia and Soloman Weeks, int. Oct. 2, 1802.

HOSKINS, Bathsheba, Mrs., of Gayhead, and Amos Jeffers, int. Oct. 4, 1849.

HOURVOIWEE (see Hawwossuee, Howwaswee), Zaccheus of Gayhead, and Elizabeth Warmsley, int. Aug. 21, 1827.

HOWLAND, Elijah of New Bedford, and Sophronia Tillton [int. Sophrona Tilton], Apr. 23 [1830].

HOWWASWEE (see Hawwossuee, Hourvoiwee), Almoth of Gayhead, and Elizabeth [int. Elisabeth] Cook, June 4, 1840.
Jane W. P. of Gayhead, and Joseph Nolden, int. Oct. 5, 1847.

HUNT, Jeane and Sam[ue]ll Nickenson, July 5, 1744.*
Mary and Nathaniel Knoles, Feb. —, 1706–7.*
Sam[ue]ll and Lois Mayhew, Jan. 7, 1747.*

HUSSEY, Joseph of Edgartown, and Mehtable Johnson, int. Feb. 8, 1809.

HUXFORD, Sarah and Dan[ie]ll Dunham, Nov. 19, 1739.*

JAFFERS (see Jeffers), Sally of Gayhead, and Samuel Peters, int. Oct. 4, 1839.

JAMES, Henry of Tisbury, and Mary Peters, int. Apr. 9, 1831.
Mary C. of Chriastiontown [int. Christiantown], and John A. Spencer, Aug. 25, 1835.

JARED, Josiah and Mrs. Olive Mingo, int. Nov. 22, 1844.

JEFFERS (see Jaffers), Amos and Bethiah Cooper, int. Jan. 15, 1806.

* Intention not recorded.

CHILMARK MARRIAGES.

JEFFERS, Amos of Gayhead, and Mrs. Bathsheba Hoskins, int. Oct. 4, 1849.
Parnel of Gayhead, and John Divine, int. May 2, 1834.

JEFFREY, William of Christiantown, and Laura Johnson, int. Apr. 21, 1832.

JENKINS, Abigail of Edgartown, and James Skiff, Oct. 26, 1775.*
Joseph [int. of Vt.] and Susan Robinson, Jan. 13, 1828.
Lemuel of Edgartown, and Elizabeth Mayhew, Aug. 20, 1775.*
Marshall of Edgartown, and Elizabeth Mayhew, Dec. 16, 1777.*

JERNIGAN, William Jr. of Edgartown, and Abigail Mayhew, Sept. 20, 1781 [dup. 1780].*

JOHNSON, Abiah and John Salsbury, int. Dec. 20, 1825.
Elizabeth and James Cooper, int. Feb. 13, 1805.
Hannah and John De Vine, int. July 4, 1801.
Hannah and George Lord, int. June 11, 1808.
Ichabod of Falmouth, and Mehitable Weeks, Nov. 26, 1718, in Falmouth.*
Isaac Jr. and Peggy Ward, Jan. 29, 1798.*
Isaac of Gayhead, and Sarah Johnson, May 1, 1838.
Joshua and Ann Cole, int. Nov. 27, 1808.
Laura of Gayhead, and William Jeffrey, int. Apr. 21, 1832.
Margaret of Edgartown, and Elisha Tauknut, Indians, Dec. 21, 1769.*
Matilda S. and Shubel Davis, int. Mar. 19, 1836.
Mehtable and Joseph Hussey, int. Feb. 8, 1809.
Philip of N.Y., and Susan Stephen, int. Dec. 28, 1827.
Philip of Gayhead, and Mary Cook, int. May 2, 1840.
Philip and Mrs. Sarah Henry, int. Sept. 12, 1845.
Polly and Thadeus Cook, int. Oct. 19, 1805.
Prince of Gayhead, and Eliza Hazzard, int. May 8, 1835.
Samuel and Lydia Cuff, int. Nov. 20, 1808.
Sarah of Gayhead, and Isaac Johnson, May 1, 1838.

JONAS, Peggey F., Mrs., of Gayhead, and Tristram Weeks, int. June 17, 1843.

JONES (see Jons), Eben[e]z[e]r and Jean Hilman, Sept. 21, 1733.*
Jone and Prince Skiff, June —, 1775.*
Sukey and Silas Hillman, Nov. 21, 1798.*
Zerviah and Ezra Hilman, Dec. 4, 1766.*

* Intention not recorded.

CHILMARK MARRIAGES.

JONS (see Jones), Mary and Robert Cathcart, Dec. 11, 1755.*

KNOLES (see Knowles), Nathaniel of Eastham, and Mary Hunt, Feb. —, 1706-7.*

KNOWLES (see Knoles), Abraham [int. Abram] of Addison, and Prudence Hillman, July 9, 1807.

LAKE, Mary E. [int. C.], 18, d. Otis and Mary, and Willard Bessey, Feb. 1, 1846.

LAMBERT (see Lumbart, Lumbert, Lumbut).

LAURENCE, Remember of Falmouth, and Nathan Weeks, Aug. 10, 1737, in Falmouth.*
William of Falmouth, and Hannah Allen, Nov. 5 [1801].

LEBARON, Lemuel of Metepoice, and Elizabeth Allen, Dec. 29, 1774.*

LEWIS, Waren of Tisbury, and Keziah Hawks, int. May 8, 1802.

LITTLE, Thomas, Dr., and Lucy Mayhew, Dec. 13, 1733.*

LOOK, Alfred, 25, of Tisbury, s. Mayhew and Mary of Tisbury, and Jane M. Cottle, July 20, 1845.
Almira and John Clifford, Aug. 14, 1827.
Daniel of Addison [int. of Addington], and Lois Hillman, Oct. 7, 1804.
Davis A. and Abigail N. Dunham, int. Nov. 9, 1826.
Eunice and Samuel Norton, July 11, 1811.*
George of Tisbury, and Persis [int. Percy] Allen, Nov. 27 [1800].
Henry W. of Tisbury, and Sophia Tilton, Mar. 8, 1848.*
James, 40, s. George and Perres, and Irenea W. [int. Irena, omits W.] Cottle, Oct. 6, 1846.
Joseph of Tisbury, and Ruth Tillton, Dec. 31, 1767.*
Lucy of Tisbury, and Maletiah Mayhew, Oct. 18, 1804.*
Martha of Tisbury, and Moses Adams, Mar. 24, 1799, in Tisbury.*
Prince of Tisbury, and Sarah Lumbart, Nov. 29, 1787.*
Rebeccah of Tisbury, and Ephraim Allen Jr., int. Mar. 1, 1807.
Robert and Enice Hillman, May 30, 1779.*
Samuel Jr. of Tisbury, and Mrs. Nancy Hillman, int. Mar. 6, 1808.
Thankful of Tisbury, and William Adams, Jan. 14, 1795, in Tisbury.*

* Intention not recorded.

CHILMARK MARRIAGES. 59

LORD, George and Hannah Johnson, int. June 11, 1808.*

LUCE, Abby A. of Tisbury, and William C. West, int. May 19, 1849.
Abigail [int. Abagail], 34, d. Daniel [and] Abigail, and Joseph Luce, June 10, 1846.
Benja[mi]n of Tisbury, and Sarah White, Aug. 25, 1774.*
Benj[amin] Jr. and Prudence Pease, Aug. 14, 1791.*
Content A. of Tisbury, and Frederick B. Skiff, int. Mar. 19, 1835.
Daniel and Abigail Holister, int. Sept. 16, 1803.
Deborah of Tisbury, and William Ferguson, Dec. 11, 1793, in Tisbury.*
Edwin A., Capt. [int. of Tisbury], and Celina Hillman, July 16, 1837.
Francis N. of Tisbury, and Bathsheba Hillman, Nov. 15, 1831.
Hannah and Mayhew Norton, July 6, 1797.*
Ira F. of Tisbury, and Eliza Hillman, Mar. 1, 1836.
Jabez of Tisbury, and Reliance Nicolls Jr., int. Apr. 3, 1802.
Joseph, 38, b. Tisbury, of Tisbury, s. Joseph and Elizabeth of Tisbury, and Abigail [int. Abagail] Luce, June 10, 1846.
Keziah and Jonathan Hilman, June 29, 1749.*
Lovey of Tisbury, and Lot Hillman, June 20, 1780, in Tisbury.*
Lydia of Tisbury, and Bartlett Pease, Jan. 22, 1795, in Tisbury.*
Mary C. [dup. 23], d. David [and] Polly, and Henry Mantor [dup. and int. Manter], Dec. —, 1843.
Rollin of Tisbury, and Tamson Mayhew, ——— [int. Aug. 15, 1828].*
Ulissus P. of Tisbury, and Mary A. Tilton, int. Mar. 12, 1831.
Warren of Tisbury, and Salley West, Oct. 19, 1797.*
Zacheus and Sarah Sog, Aug. 10, 1749.*

LUMBART (see Lumbert, Lumbut), Sarah and Prince Look, Nov. 29, 1787.*

LUMBERT (see Lumbart, Lumbut), Abisha Haden (Lumber[t]) and Hephsabah Coffin, Oct. 16, 1792.*
Bathshaba and William Pool, May 17, 1798.*
Deborah and Isaac Winslow, Nov. 20 [1800].
Deborah P. and Capt. George P. Manter, int. Apr. 14, 1849.
Jerusha and Jonathan Mosieur, July 4, 1776.*
Jonathan (Lumb[e]r[t]) and Rachel Tilton, Oct. 19, 1707.*
Jonathan and Love Manter, Nov. 19 [1800].
Keziah [dup. and int. Kaziah] F. and Samuel Flanders, Apr. 2, 1837.

* Intention not recorded.

CHILMARK MARRIAGES.

LUMBERT, Lemel (Lumb[e]r[t]) and Relian[c]e Cottel, Oct. 14, 1756.*
Mary and Jeremiah Stewart, Nov. 6, 1788.*
Sarah and Isaiah Hillman, int. Jan. 3, 1846.
Sophrona P. and John Pease Jr., Jan. 3, 1830.
Thomas and Parnell Hillman, Oct. 30, 1791.*
William M. of Tisbury, and Betsey W. Hancock, Oct. 30, 1828.

LUMBUT (see Lumbart, Lumbert), Thomas H. and Deborah A. ———, Nov. 26, 1817.* [Lambert, Nov. 26, 1818, G.R.]
Thomas H. and Lydia West, Jan. 22, 1825.*

MACCOMBER, Simeon A. and Nancy W. Robinson, int. Aug. 1, 1840.

MADISON, Michael of Edgartown, and Diana Peters, June 2, 1830.*

MAGEE (see Megee).

MANING (see Manning), Abiah of Gayhead, and Nathan F. Cooper, int. May 27, 1837.

MANN, Thomas P. [int. omits P.] of New Bedford, and Eliza Gifford, Apr. 6, 1831.

MANNING (see Maning), Abel of Gayhead, and Almira Cook, May 24, 1844.
Hannah, Mrs., of Gayhead, and George W. Gardner, int. Feb. 24, 1838.
Marshall and Hannah Tocknet, int. Apr. 7, 1810.
Mary of Gayhead, and William [int. Williams] L. Brooks, July 26, 1839.

MANTER (see Mantor), George P., Capt., of Tisbury, and Deborah P. Lumbert, int. Apr. 14, 1849.
Granville, Capt., and Catharine C. Mayhew, int. Oct. 27, 1838.
Jane, Mrs. [int. 34], and Capt. Daniel Flanders, Mar. 5, 1843.
Love of Tisbury, and Jonathan Lumbert, Nov. 19 [1800].
Samuel, Capt., and Mrs. Sarah Cox, int. Nov. 14, 1801.
Sanderson and Jane H. Mayhew, int. Sept. 27, 1834.

MANTOR (see Manter), Henry [dup. and int. 30] of Tisbury, s. Thomas [and] Hannah, and Mary C. Luce, Dec. —, 1843.
Thankful, 21, d. Whitten and Thankful, and Cyrus Hancock, Dec. 26, 1844.

* Intention not recorded.

MARCH (see Marche), Wilson [and] Abigal Allen, Dec. 9, 1748.*

MARCHE (see March), Joanna and Timothy Robinson, July 7, 1762.*

MAYHEW, Abagal and Jonathan Allen, Nov. 17, 1733.*
Abiah and Daniel Norton, May 31, 1787.*
Abiah, d. Thomas, and William Tilton, ———.*
Abigail and William Jernigan Jr., Sept. 20, 1781 [dup. 1780].*
Abigail and Davis Cottle, int. Apr. 8, 1837.
Abner [int. Jr.] and Eunice Smith, Nov. 5, 1807.
Allen, Dr., and Eunice Allen, Dec. 18, 1795.*
Asenath P. [int. W. [?]] and Thomas Clifford, July 23, 1836.
Bartlet and Thankful Mayhew, int. Oct. 6, 1826.
Beersheba [dup. Bathsheba, d. Dea. Timothy] and Will[ia]m Tillton [dup. Tilton], Jan. 14, 1762.*
Benjamen and Hannah Skiff, May 13, 1704.*
Benjamin and Lidia Mayhew, Feb. 8, 1784.*
Benjamin [dup. and int. 56], s. Benjamin [and] Lydia, and Hannah Smith, Nov. 23, 1843.
Bethia and Jacob Norton Jr., Feb. 3, 1731-2.*
Bethiah and William Clerk, Sept. 4, 1707.*
Caroline and Capt. William Mayhew [int. Jr.], Aug. 14, 1834.
Catharine C. and Capt. Granville Manter, int. Oct. 27, 1838.
Clarissa [dup. Clarrissa] and Tristram Allen, Dec. 17, 1795.*
David and Martha Mayhew Jr., int. Sept. 26, 1802.
Deborah and Abel Baker, Aug. 23, 1795.*
Deborah and James Mayhew, int. Oct. 30, 1830.
Deidamia S. and Joseph Mayhew Jr., Sept. 15, 1839.
Edward, 26, s. George and Clarissa, and Jane A. Swett, June 26, 1845.
Elijah and Eunice Norton, June 11, 1729.*
Elijah and Martha Mayhew, int. Oct. 10, 1835.
Elijah L., 59, s. Melitiah and Lucy, and Asenath M. Norton, Apr. 18, 1847.
Eliza L. [int. 19], d. Abner [and] Eunice, and Josiah Mayhew, May 25, 1843.
Elizabeth and Lemuel Jenkins, Aug. 20, 1775.*
Elizabeth and Marshall Jenkins, Dec. 16, 1777.*
Elliz[a]beth and Josiah Tilton, Feb. 23, 1743.*
Ephraim Jr. and Susanna [int. Susannah] Pease, Feb. 13, 1805.
Ephraim Jr. and Lucinda Pool, Nov. 24, 1836.*
Experience and Remember Bourne, Dec. 4, 1711.*
Francis and Sophronia Smith, Dec. 11, 1788.*

* Intention not recorded.

MAYHEW, Frederick and Mary Blackwell, int. Jan. 15, 1836.
George and Mehitable [int. Mehiteble] Mayhew, Oct. 7, 1830.
Hannah and Zephaniah Mayhew, Oct. 23, 1735.*
Hannah and Elijah Smith, Aug. 14, 1768.*
Hannah D., 17, d. Davis and Cynthia, and Oliver Mayhew, May 28, 1845.
Hariff [int. Harriph] and Sally Smith, July 4, 1832.
Hebron and Deborah Stewart, [Sept.] 20 [?], 1792.*
Hilyard and Susanna Bassett, Feb. 16, 1764.*
James and Deborah Mayhew, int. Oct. 30, 1830.
James and Caroline Cottle, int. June 27, 1835.
Jane H. and Sanderson Manter, int. Sept. 27, 1834.
Jean and John Bassett, July 31, 1735.*
Jedidah and Joseph Mayhew, int. June 7, 1803.
Jemima and Thomas Tillton, Dec. 9, 1725.*
Jeremiah Jr. and Abigail Bassett, Mar. 3, 1768.*
Jeremiah and Fear Hillman, Apr. 7, 1776.*
Jeremiah, Capt., of New Bedford, and Mrs. Peggy Mayhew, [Oct.] 26, 1792.*
John Jr. and Hannah Gray, Jan. 15, 1783, in Tisbury.*
Jonathan and Parnell Mayhew, Oct. 25, 1792.*
Jonathan and Jane S. Pool, June 26, 1842.
Joseph and Jedidah Mayhew, int. June 7, 1803.
Joseph Jr. and Deidamia S. Mayhew, Sept. 15, 1839.
Josiah and Rebecca Skiffe, Oct. 21, 1779.*
Josiah [int. 28], s. Melatiah [and] Lucy, and Eliza L. Mayhew, May 25, 1843.
Julina T. and William Rogers, Apr. 4, 1841.
Keziah and Dan[ie]ll Butler, Oct. 8, 1730.*
Lidia and Benjamin Mayhew, Feb. 8, 1784.*
Lois and Sam[ue]ll Hunt, Jan. 7, 1747.*
Louisa and Herman Vincent, Nov. 6, 1831.
Lucinda and Levi Davis, int. Mar. 2, 1827.
Lucy and Dr. Thomas Little, Dec. 13, 1733.*
Lucy and Willi[a]m Mayhew, Dec. 31, 1772.*
Lucy and Charles Norton, int. Mar. 24, 1828.
Maletiah and Lucy Look, int. Oct. 18, 1804.
Martha and Shubil Smith Jr., Jan. —, 1723-4.*
Martha and Silvanus Parker, Dec. 9, 1749.*
Martha Jr. and David Mayhew, int. Sept. 26, 1802.
Martha and Capt. Allen Dexter, int. Mar. 2, 1827.
Martha [int. adds Mrs.] and Capt. [int. omits Capt.] Samuel Blackwell, Aug. —, 1833.

* Intention not recorded.

CHILMARK MARRIAGES. 63

MAYHEW, Martha and Elijah Mayhew, int. Oct. 10, 1835.
Mary and Jethro Athearn, Sept. 8, 1720.*
Mary [dup. d. Matthew] and Beriah Tillton [dup. Tilton], Dec. 12, 1728.*
Mary and Peleg Burrig, Sept. 20, 1742.*
Mary and John Allen, Oct. 17, 1777.*
Matilda and Elijah Smith, [Aug.] 28, 1791.*
Matilda V. and Charles F. Dunham, int. June 6, 1840.
Matthew and Mary ———, Mar. 1, 1674.*
Matthew and Mary Allen, Jan. 3, 1744.*
Mehitable [int. Mehiteble] and George Mayhew, Oct. 7, 1830.
Mercy and Abil Chase, Feb. 14, 1744.*
Mercy and Ephraim Smith, Oct. 2 [1800].*
Moses and Rebecca Mayhew, Nov. 28, 1824.*
Nancy S. and John Dunham, Aug. 6, 1839.
Nathan and Abigail Bordman, Nov. 8, 1781.*
Nathaniel and Mary Athearn, Feb. 20, 1784, in Tisbury.*
Olive and David Davis, Nov. 30, 1786.*
Oliver and Jane Stewart, May 26, 1791.*
Oliver, 27, s. Malitiah and Lucy, and Hannah D. Mayhew, May 28, 1845.
Pain and Mary Rankin, Dec. 8, 1699.*
Pain Jr. and Dinah Norton, Dec. 1, 1724.*
Pain Jr. and Margate Wass, Nov. 17, 1757.*
Parnell and Jonathan Mayhew, Oct. 25, 1792.*
Peggy and Will[ia]m Mayhew, Jan. 7, 1773.*
Peggy, Mrs., and Capt. Jeremiah Mayhew, [Oct.] 26, 1792.*
Phebe, Mrs., and William Mayhew, Jan. 1, 1795.*
Phebe and David L. Adams, int. May 26, 1826.
Polly and Ephraim Poole, Oct. 18, 1804.
Priscilla and Nathan Bassett, Oct. 29, 1828.
Prudence and Zebulon [dup. Sibulon] Allen, May 7, 1789.*
Rebecca and Mayhew Adams, Dec. 27, 1750.*
Rebecca and Rufus Davis, Dec. 4, 1794.*
Rebecca and Moses Mayhew, Nov. 28, 1824.*
Reliance and Benj[ami]n Hatch, Jan. 14, 1762.*
Sarah and Abishai Folger, Nov. 6, 1727.*
Sarah and W[illia]m Allen, Nov. 13, 1737 [dup. 1739, *sic*].*
Seth and Mercy Skiff, Dec. 15, 1763.*
Seth and Elizabeth [int. Betcy] Cottle, June 4 [1801].
Simon and Abiah Vinson, Apr. 27, 1749.*
Simon and Matilda Vinson, Apr. 21, 1796.*
Smith and Thankful V. Cotte, int. Feb. 3, 1827.

* Intention not recorded.

CHILMARK MARRIAGES.

MAYHEW, Sorah and Henry Hillman, [Dec.] 9, 1790.*
Susanah and Silas Hilman, Dec. 4, 1755.*
Susanna and Ransom Norton, [Mar.] 27, 1791.*
Tamson and Rollin Luce, ——— [int. Aug. 15, 1828].*
Thankful and Bartlet Mayhew, int. Oct. 6, 1826.
Theophilus and Elizabeth Tillton, Feb. 22, 1776.*
Thomas T. and Mrs. Mary Hancock, int. May 3, 1845.
Thomas Waid and Parnal Adams, Dec. 21, 1780.*
Timothy and Abiah Tilton, Jan. 14, 1730–1.*
Tristram [int. Tristra], 39, s. David and Martha, and Jane Nickerson [int. Nickenson], Nov. 25, 1849.
Wadsworth and Elizabeth Gregrey, Oct. 5, 1775.*
Willi[a]m of Edgartown, and Lucy Mayhew, Dec. 31, 1772.*
Will[ia]m and Peggy Mayhew, Jan. 7, 1773.*
William and Mrs. Phebe Mayhew, Jan. 1, 1795.*
William [int. adds Jr.], Capt., and Caroline Mayhew, Aug. 14, 1834.
Will[ia]m B. [int. Brandon] and Prudence Allen [dup. Jr.], Nov. 6 [1800].
William L. and Sarah C. Merry, int. July 6, 1844.
Willmut and Nancy Tillton, Oct. 27, 1785.*
Zaccheus [dup. Zach[eu]s] and Rebecca [dup. Rebeckah] Pope, Sept. 6, 1750.*
Zephaniah and Bethyah Wadsworth, Mar. —, 1711.*
Zephaniah and Hannah Mayhew, Oct. 23, 1735.*
Zephaniah [and] Polite Wadsworth, Nov. 24, 1773, in Tisbury.*
Zilpah and Joseph Tilton, Apr. 15, 1742.*

McCOLLUM, Archabald and Patty Godfrey, Apr. 24 [1800].*
Mary E. [int. McCullum, omits E.] and Capt. Allen Tillton, Apr. 20, 1834.

MEADER, William of Nontuckett, and Deborah Skiff, Oct. 20, 1774.*

MEGEE, Jean and Edward Carturight, Jan. 1, 1749.*

MEIGS (see Miggs).

MERRY (see Mery), Benj[ami]n and Hannah Skiff, Oct. 23, 1740.*
Benjamin of Tisbury, and Rebecca [int. Rebeca] Robinson, Apr. 17 [int. Apr. 24, *sic*], 1835.
James L., 30, b. Tisbury, of Tisbury, s. Matthew and Betsey of Tisbury, and Emily A. Cottle, Oct. 7 [? 11], 1846.

* Intention not recorded.

CHILMARK MARRIAGES.

MERRY, John and Mehetabel Hilman, ———.*
Larthrop [int. of Tisbury] and Abigal Pease, Dec. 26, 1805.
Malachi of Tisbury, and Rhoda Hilman, June 26, 1766.*
Sarah C. of Tisbury, and William L. Mayhew, int. July 6, 1844.

MERY (see Merry), Abigal and Sam[ue]ll Cottle, Oct. 23, 1724.*

MIGGS, Martha of Falmouth, and Jabez Robinson, Feb. 25, 1768, in Falmouth.*

MILLS, John and Bathsheba Allen, Oct. 31, 1726.*

MINGO (see Mingoe), Charles of Tisbury, and Mrs. Sarah Goodwin, int. May 6, 1837.
Olive, Mrs., of Gayhead, and Josiah Jared, int. Nov. 22, 1844.

MINGOE (see Mingo), Samuel of Tisbury, and Hannah Cuffe, Aug. 21, 1831.

MITCHEL, William and Prudence West, int. Feb. 2, 1833.

MOSIEUR, Jonathan and Jerusha Lumbert, July 4, 1776.*

MOULTON, Hannah and Samuel Tilton, ———.*

NEVERS, David T. [int. Daniel F.] of Gayhead, and Mrs. Anna Cooper, Jan. 1, 1843.

NICHOLS (see Nicolls), Betsey and Freeman Gray, Oct. 11, 1798.*

NICHOLSON (see Nickenson, Nickerson), Abigail [dup. Nickerson] and Benjamin Bassett [dup. Bassitt], Jan. 22, 1778.*
Nathaniel and Lydia Hillman, Sept. 21, 1780.*

NICKENSON (see Nicholson, Nickerson), Sam[ue]ll and Jeane Hunt, July 5, 1744.*

NICKERSON (see Nicholson, Nickenson), Jane and Robert Thompson, Jan. 15, 1768.*
Jane [int. Nickenson], 19, d. Samuel and Cevies [Clarissa], and Tristram [int. Tristra] Mayhew, Nov. 25, 1849.
Samuel and Clarissa [dup. Clarrissa] Hillman, May 17, 1829.

NICOLLS (see Nichols), Reliance Jr. and Jabez Luce, int. Apr. 3, 1802.

NOLDEN, Joseph of Surnam, W. Indieas, and Jane W. P. Howwaswee, int. Oct. 5, 1847.

* Intention not recorded.

NORTEN (see Norton), Freeman and Martha Chipman, Apr. 19, 1774.*

NORTON (see Norten), Asenath M., 25, b. Delhi Township, O., d. Tristram and Mary, and Elijah L. Mayhew, Apr. 18, 1847.
Bartlet of Edgartown, and Margaret Tilton, int. Dec. 28, 1827.
Catharine S. and George Fifield, int. Feb. 26, 1842.
Charles of Industry, Me., and Lucy Mayhew, int. Mar. 24, 1828.
Constant and Amy Cottle, Sept. 11, 1788, in Tisbury.*
Daniel and Mary Tillton, June 15, 1780.*
Daniel and Abiah Mayhew, May 31, 1787.*
Desire of Edgartown, and Robert Allen, Dec. 21, 1752 [dup. 1753, *sic*].*
Dinah and Pain Mayhew Jr., Dec. 1, 1724.*
Eliakim Esq. of Tisbury, and Mrs. [int. omits Mrs.] Martha F. Norton, Aug. —, 1842.
Eunice and Elijah Mayhew, June 11, 1729.*
Hannah of Tisbury, and James R. Tillton, int. Apr. 26, 1834.
Jacob and Mrs. Hannah Barker, June 8, 1727, in Pembrook.*
Jacob Jr. and Bethia Mayhew, Feb. 3, 1731–2.*
James Jr. and Olive Chase, Mar. 26, 1783, in Tisbury.*
Lot of Edgartown, and Deborah Hillman, Dec. 4, 1777.*
Lucy of Tisbury, and Salathiel Allen, Sept. 24, 1783, in Tisbury.*
Lucy and Nicholas [dup. Nicholos] Butler, Nov. 5, 1789.*
Lydia of Edgartown, and Nathan Bassett, Sept. 22, 1791.*
Lydia B. and James N. Tilton, int. June 17, 1837.
Martha F., Mrs. [int. omits Mrs.], and Eliakim Norton Esq., Aug. —, 1842.
Mary and Sam[ue]ll Norton, Feb. 22, 1728.*
Mary B. and Josiah Tillton, Nov. 24, 1814.*
Mary B. and Silas Hillman, July 19, 1835.
Mayhew of Tisbury, and Hannah Luce, July 6, 1797.*
Polly and Owen Hillman, Aug. 20, 1795.*
Ransom and Susanna Mayhew, [Mar.] 27, 1791.*
Samuel and Eunice Look, July 11, 1811.*
Sam[ue]ll and Mary Norton, Feb. 22, 1728.*
Shubael and Love Adams, Jan. 11, 1791.*
Shubal of Tisbury, and Mary N. [dup. omits N.] Hillman, Feb. 21, 1828.
Thomas of Edgartown, and Lovisa [int. Lovice] Adams, Oct. 26, 1806.
W[illia]m and Polly Bassett, Nov. 10, 1791.*
William and Martha G. Bassett, June 30, 1842.

* Intention not recorded.

NYE, John and Tamer Weeks, Feb. 9, 1774.*
John and Mary Price, July 9, 1797, in Falmouth.*
Moses of Sandwich, and Rhoda Butler, Nov. 11, 1792.*
Remember and Michal Daggett, int. Mar. 3, 1804.

OCAOOCH, Naoma and John Salsbury, int. Aug. 24, 1808.

PALMER, Deliverance and Lemuel Weeks, Dec. 29, 1746, in Falmouth.*

PANU, Simon [int. Painyoo of Edgartown] and Susannah Pechauher [int. Susanna Pelhaukah] [Indians], Oct. 14, 1802.
Simon and Dorcas Swasy [Indians], int. Mar. 30, 1805.

PARKER, Hepsabah of Falmouth, and Ebenezar Tilton, Jan. 6, 1785, in Falmouth.*
Isaac of Rochester, and Abiah Hatch, Sept. 10, 1773.*
Silvanus and Martha Mayhew, Dec. 9, 1749.*

PAUL (see Paull), Abiah and Recol [int. Recall] De Grass [int. [Indians]], Feb. 13, 1805.

PAULL (see Paul), Sarah, Mrs., and Joseph Henery, int. Aug. 2, 1802.

PEABARDAY (see Peabody), Pelig of Dartmoth, and Sally Pease, Sept. 8, 1799.*

PEABODY (see Peabarday), Ruth of Dartmouth, and Silas, Gifford, Mar. 23, 1788.*

PEARSE, Benjamin and Matild White, int. May 11, 1847.

PEAS (see Pease), Abigail and Benj[ami]n Burges, Feb. 25, 1740.*
John and Hannah Hillman, Feb. 22, 1776.*
Lucy and Stephen Peas, Aug. 12, 1774.*
Stephen of Edgartown, and Lucy Peas, Aug. 12, 1774.*

PEASE (see Peas), Abigal and Larthrop Merry, Dec. 26, 1805.
Abisha and Jedidah Allen, Feb. 28, 1798, in Tisbury.*
Bartlett and Lydia Luce, Jan. 22, 1795, in Tisbury.*
Fortunatus Jr. and Rose Gifferd, Nov. 28, 1788.*
Fortunatus and Susannah Sherman, wid., Jan. 14, 1800.*
Jedidah and Cornelus Tillton, Feb. 16, 1780.*
John Jr. and Sophrona P. Lumbert, Jan. 3, 1830.
Lydia and Sam[ue]l Bradford, Nov. 25, 1762.*
Nathaniel and Elizabeth Gifford, Feb. 21, 1796.*

* Intention not recorded.

CHILMARK MARRIAGES.

PEASE, Persis and Anderson Taylor, Jan. 9, 1791.*
Prudence and Benj[amin] Luce Jr., Aug. 14, 1791.*
Sally and Pelig Peabarday, Sept. 8, 1799.*
Samuel and Mercy Trapp, Jan. 4, 1710.*
Shubal and Dorcus Claghern, Nov. 5, 1761.*
Susanna [int. Susannah] and Ephraim Mayhew Jr., Feb. 13, 1805.

PECHAUHER, Susannah [int. Susanna Pelhaukah] and Simon Panu [int. Painyoo] [Indians], Oct. 14, 1802.

PECKAM (see Peckham), Clemmant and Margate Allen, Oct. 29, 1744.*

PECKHAM (see Peckam), Prince of Dartmoth, and Sarah Asten, Nov. 28, 1780.*

PERRY, Jonathan of Nantucket, and Mehitable Robinson, Jan. 6, 1796.*

PETERS, Diana and Michael Madison, June 2, 1830.*
Ele [?] of Gayhead, and Hebron Wamsley Jr., int. May 23, 1840.
Elnora of Gayhead, and Francis Salvey, int. Dec. 10, 1841.
Francis of Edgartown, and Hepsabah Amos, int. Dec. 9, 1807.
Hannah of Gayhead, and Jonathan Cuff, Apr. 12, 1843.
Johnson of Edgartown, and Molly Ephraim, int. Nov. 4, 1807.
Lucy of Gayhead, and Aaron Cooper Jr., int. May 30, 1840.
Mary of Gayhead, and Henry James, int. Apr. 9, 1831.
Nathaniel and Mary Dodge, int. Oct. 12, 1806.
Samuel of Gayhead, and Sally Jaffers, int. Oct. 4, 1839.
Sophia of Gayhead, and George Belane, int. Oct. 16, 1835.

PIERCE (see Pearse).

POND, Calo and Margaret Dodge, int. Aug. 28, 1807.

POOL (see Poole), Jane S. [int. 24] and Jonathan Mayhew, June 26, 1842.
Levina A., 22, and Capt. Austin Smith, Nov. 30, 1842.
Lucinda and Ephraim Mayhew Jr., Nov. 24, 1836.*
Matthew and Martha A. [int. Ann] Adams, Aug. 27, 1834.
Parnal and Capt. Richard Flanders, June 6, 1832.
William and Bathshaba Lumbert, May 17, 1798.*

POOLE (see Pool), Ephraim and Polly Mayhew, Oct. 18, 1804.
Mary and William West, int. Nov. 12, 1808.
Will[ia]m and Mary Burges, Dec. 10, 1767.*

* Intention not recorded.

POPE, Mercy of Dartmouth, and Caleb Church, Jan. 29, 1752.*
Rebecca [dup. Rebeckah] of Dartmouth, and Zaccheus [dup. Zach[eu]s] Mayhew, Sept. 6, 1750.*

PORRIGE, Mercy [? Dorrige] and Charls Harison, Feb. 20, 1800.*

POTTER, ———, Adml., of Dartmouth, and Ann Skiff Jr., Nov. 16, 1774.*

PRENTICE (see Printice).

PRICE, Mary of Falmouth, and John Nye, July 9, 1797, in Falmouth.*

PRINCE, Hannah of Falmouth, and Barnabas Robinson, Sept. 3, 1789, in Falmouth.*
Mercy and Shubil Weeks, Feb. 7, 1710.*

PRINTICE, Mary Ann, Mrs. [int. of Stoneington, Conn.], and John Davis, Apr. 13, 1843.

QUAPISH, Alice of Masshpee, and Thomas Francis, int. Aug. 11, 1827.

RANKIN, Mary and Pain Mayhew, Dec. 8, 1699.*

REED, Lemuel B. [int. R.], 23, b. Dartmouth, of Dart[mouth], s. Lemuel and Faley of Dartmouth, and Sophronia W. Cottle, Nov. 6, 1846.
Rodney R., 21, b. Dartmouth, of Westport, s. Lemuel and **Faley** of Dartmouth, and Prudence Cottle, Nov. 6, 1846.

RICHARDSON, Benj[amin] of Unity, and Sylvia Hawks, Mar. 24, 1791.*

RIPLEY, Abigail J. and Capt. Francis C. Smith, int. Apr. 10, 1841.
Henry Jr. [int. 25, of Edgartown] and Cynthia Smith, Nov. 24, 1842.

ROBENSON (see Robinson), Zepheniah and Anna Hatch, Feb. 27, 1757, in Falmouth.*

ROBERSON, Martha and Matthew [int. Mathew] P. Butler, Oct. 29, 1835.

ROBINSON (see Robenson), Abigail and Isaac Daggett, int. Dec. 15, 1838.
Anna H. and W. Chamberlin, Sept. 25, 1825.*

* Intention not recorded.

CHILMARK MARRIAGES.

ROBINSON, Anne and Matthew Tillton Jr., int. Aug. 12, 1803.
Barnabas and Hannah Prince, Sept. 3, 1789, in Falmouth.*
Cornelius and Fear Gifford, Apr. 21, 1792.*
Deborah and Shadrach Robinson, Dec. 6, 1779.*
Edmand and Fear Robinson, Jan. 17, 1782.*
Elihu and Sarah Sandford, Nov. 22, 1762.*
Elihu and Huldah Gifford, Sept. 8, 1779, in Falmouth.*
Eliza and Thomas Taskir, int. Jan. 9, 1827.
Fear and Edmand Robinson, Jan. 17, 1782.*
Hannah and Phineus Butler, Mar. 3, 1743.*
Hannah and Jeremiah Butler, Nov. 14, 1781.*
Henry and Luretia Adams, Mar. 15, 1827.
Isaac and Mary Robinson, Jan. 16, 1760, in Tisbury.*
Jabez and Martha Miggs, Feb. 25, 1768, in Falmouth.*
Jedidah and David Tilton [int. Tillton], Sept. 25, 1806.
Jeremiah and Abigal Green, —— 9, 1757.*
John and Jane Allen, July 25, 1807.
Mary and Isaac Robinson, Jan. 16, 1760, in Tisbury.*
Mary and Daniel P. Gifford, Nov. 18, 1830.
Mehitable and Jonathan Perry, Jan. 6, 1796.*
Nancy W. and Simeon A. Maccomber, int. Aug. 1, 1840.
Paul and Nabby Weeks, int. Oct. 5, 1804.
Phebe Ann [int. Anne] and Allen W. Durfee, —— [int. Sept. 24], 1831.
Rebecca [int. Rebeca] and Benjamin Merry, Apr. 17 [int. Apr. 24, sic], 1835.
Samuel and Rebecca Weeks, Aug. 4, 1780, in Falmouth.*
Shadrach and Deborah Robinson, Dec. 6, 1779.*
Sophronia and Beriah Austin, Oct. 1, 1826.*
Stephen and Polly Gifford, June 22, 1796.*
Susan and Joseph Jenkins, Jan. 13, 1828.
Susannah and Edward Austin, Dec. 21, 1778.*
Temperance S. [int. Patience] and Sanford Herendeen, N[ov.] 18, 1827.
Timothy and Joanna Marche, July 7, 1762.*
Zephanieh Jr. of Nashon, and Hannah Davis, July 29, 1787, in Falmouth.*

ROCH (see Rotch), Olive of Tisbury, and Whitten Hillman, Sept. 2, 1784, in Tisbury.*

ROGERS, Esther of Gayhead, and Nathan Francis Jr. [dup. omits Jr.], Feb. 26, 1795.*
William of Tisbury, and Julina T. Mayhew, Apr. 4, 1841.

* Intention not recorded.

ROSE (see Rows), Isaac A. of Gayhead, and Harriet A. Wamslay, int. Apr. 5, 1841.

ROTCH (see Roch), John D. and Sarah Tilton, Oct. 28, 1828.
Nancy and Thomas Smith [int. Jr.], Mar. 17, 1831.

ROWS (see Rose), Isaac of New Bedford, and Priscilla Womsley, int. May 23, 1837.

RUSSEL (see Russell), Lydia of Tisbury, and Mayhew Adams, Dec. 13, 1792, in Tisbury.*
Will[ia]m of Dartmouth, and Patience Swain, Mar. 2, 1773.*

RUSSELL (see Russel), Holder of Dartmouth [dup. Darthmouth], and Deborah Slocum [dup. Slocomb], Aug. 15, 1791.*

SAILSBURY (see Salsbury), Emily of Gay Head, and Thaddeus Cook, int. Oct. 4, 1849.

SALSBURY (see Sailsbury), John and Naoma Ocaooch, int. Aug. 24, 1808.
John and Abiah Johnson, int. Dec. 20, 1825.

SALVEY, Francis of Edgartown, and Elnora Peters, int. Dec. 10, 1841.

SAMSON, Ann of Darthmouth, and Shubel Smith, Oct. 12, 1725.

SANDFORD (see Sanford), Sarah and Elihu Robinson, Nov. 22, 1762.*

SANFORD (see Sandford), Elizabeth and Christopher Almy, Dec. 30, 1762.*

SHEPHERD, William of Tisbury, and Clarissa Cooper, int. May 21, 1841.

SHERMAN, Abigail of Dartmouth, Bristol Co., and Silvanus C[o]ttle, Feb. 18, 1745.*
Susannah, wid., of Dartmouth, and Fortunatus Pease, Jan. 14, 1800.*

SKIFF (see Skiffe), Abigail and Jacob Skiff, Nov. 4, 1802.
Ann Jr. and Adml. ——— Potter, Nov. 16, 1774.*
Bathsheba and Jacob Clifford, Nov. 8, 1742.*
Bathsheba [int. Bersheba] and Stephen Hillman, Apr. 24, 1806.

* Intention not recorded.

SKIFF, Benj[amin] Jr. and Susanah Hillman, Dec. 12, 1765.*
Charles M., 25 [dup. s. Stephen [and] Bathsheba], and Chatharine [dup. Chatherine] M. Tilton, Apr. 4, 1844.
Deborah and William Meader, Oct. 20, 1774.*
Ebenezar and Deborah Ellis, Dec. 29, 1791, in Plymouth.*
Frederick B. and Content A. Luce, int. Mar. 19, 1835.
Hannah and Benjamen Mayhew, May 13, 1704.*
Hannah and Benj[ami]n Merry, Oct. 23, 1740.*
Jacob of New Bedford, and Abigail Skiff, Nov. 4, 1802.
James and Abigail Jenkins, Oct. 26, 1775.*
Joseph and Remember Gibs, July 7, 1740.*
Mary [dup. Skiffe] and Thomas Bacon [dup. Bakon], Sept. 7, 1721.*
Mary and Samuel Skiff, Jan. 27, 1769.*
Matty and David Tillton, Feb. 27, 1800.*
Mercy and Seth Mayhew, Dec. 15, 1763.*
Nathan and Mercy Chipman, Dec. 13, 1699, in Sandwich.*
Nathan and Margaret Warldred, Mar. 13, 1766.*
Prince and Jone Jones, June —, 1775.*
Rebecca and Charles Tilton, Nov. 22, 1840.
Samuel and Mary Skiff, Jan. 27, 1769.*
Sarah and David Smith, Jan. 22, 1778.*
Stephen and Bathsheba Tilton, Aug. 26, 1742.*
Stephen D. and Polly C. Tilton, Feb. 3, 1842.
Vinal and Cathrine Tillton, Nov. 11, 1779.*

SKIFFE (see Skiff), Abigail and Zepheniah Chase, Oct. 10, 1773.*
Rebecca and Josiah Mayhew, Oct. 21, 1779.*

SLOCUM, Deborah [dup. Slocomb] and Holder Russell, Aug. 15, 1791.*
Mary of Dartmouth, and Holder Allen, int. Mar. 31, 1832.
Oliver and Lydia Cheney, Sept. 7, 1792.*

SMITH, Austin, Capt., 30, and Levina A. Pool, Nov. 30, 1842.
Benjamin and Ruhamah Tillton, Aug. 22, 1793.*
Catharine [int. Katharine] and Lott Cottle, Sept. 30, 1804.
Charlotte and Daniel Flanders, Jan. 24, 1830.
Cynthia [int. 22] and Henry Ripley Jr., Nov. 24, 1842.
David of Edgartown, and Sarah Skiff, Jan. 22, 1778.*
Elijah of Edgartown, and Hannah Mayhew, Aug. 14, 1768.*
Elijah and Matilda Mayhew, [Aug.] 28, 1791.*
Ephraim of New Sharon, and Mercy Mayhew, Oct. 2 [1800].*

* Intention not recorded.

CHILMARK MARRIAGES. 73

SMITH, Eunice and Abner Mayhew [int. Jr.], Nov. 5, 1807.
Francis C., Capt., and Abigail J. Ripley, int. Apr. 10, 1841.
George A. and Betsey A. Allen, int. Aug. 19, 1837.
Hannah, 38, of Lowell [dup. Lowel] [dup. d. Benjamin [and] Rhuhamah], and Benjamin Mayhew, Nov. 23, 1843.
Jonathan, Rev., and Anna Williams, Oct. 25, 1789.*
Mary and Thomas Brown, Apr. 1, 1832.
Mayhew and Sarah Cottle, int. Mar. 12, 1803.
Otis and Jain [int. Jane] N. Hillman, Oct. 30, 1833.
Rufus N. and Patience G. Chase, Aug. —, 1843.
Sally and Harriff [int. Harriph] Mayhew, July 4, 1832.
Sarah and Asa Tillton, Mar. 19 [1801].
Shubel and Ann Samson, Oct. 12, 1725.
Shubil Jr. and Martha Mayhew, Jan. —, 1723-4.*
Sophronia and Francis Mayhew, Dec. 11, 1788.*
Thomas [int. Jr.] of Edgartown, and Nancy Rotch, Mar. 17, 1831.

SOG, Sarah and Zacheus Luce, Aug. 10, 1749.*

SPANIARD, Betcy and Thomas Francis, int. May 23, 1800.

SPAULDING, Sophia of Tisbury, and Henry Allen, Feb. 19, 1801.

SPENCER, John A. of New Bedford, and Mary C. James, Aug. 25, 1835.

SPOFFORD, Mary S., 25, d. Luke A. C., and John R. Wiltsic, widr. [int. omits widr.], Jan. 9, 1845.

SPRAGUE, Margaret W., d. Joseph and w., and John Cottle, Nov. 23, 1847 [int. 1877, *sic*].
Mary M., 21, d. Joseph and Harriet, and William H. Crowell [int. Crowel], July 21, 1846.
William F. and Martha L. Daggett, int. Aug. 13, 1847.

STEPHEN (see Stephens), Susan of Gayhead, and Philip Johnson, int. Dec. 28, 1827.

STEPHENS (see Stephen), Joshua of Sandwich, and Esther Tockanet, int. Mar. 7, 1801.

STEWART (see Stewort, Stuart), Charissa [dup. Carrissa] and Norton Bassett, [Sept.] 22 [dup. Sept. 12], 1791.*
Deborah and Hebron Mayhew, [Sept.] 20 [?], 1792.*

* Intention not recorded.

STEWART, George W. and Jerusha T. Cottle, Sept. 15, 1831.
Jane and Oliver Mayhew, May 26, 1791.*
Jeremiah and Mary Lumbert, Nov. 6, 1788.*
Katharine and Thomas Butler, Apr. 5, 1776.*
Margaret, d. William and Ruhamah, and William Tilton, ———.*

STEWORT (see Stewart, Stuart), W[illia]m and Bathsheba Tillton, Sept. 17, 1789.*

STODARD, Ichabod and Deborah Church, Aug. 9, 1749.*

STUART (see Stewart, Stewort), John and Lydia Cottel, Dec. 24, 1772.*
Thankful and Joseph Vinson, July 10, 1766.*
Timothy and Thankfull Dunham, ———, 1763.*

SWAIN, Patience and Will[ia]m Russel, Mar. 2, 1773.*

SWASY, Dorcas and Simon Panu [Indians], int. Mar. 30, 1805.

SWETT, Jane A., 19, d. Naum and Abbiah, and Edward Mayhew, June 26, 1845.

TABER, Vincent of Fairhaven, and Lovey West, int. Apr. 7, 1827.
Vincent and Sidney [female] Tillton, Mar. 28, 1833.

TASKIR, Thomas and Eliza Robinson, int. Jan. 9, 1827.

TAUKNUT (see Tockanet, Tocknet, Tockquenett), Elisha and Margaret Johnson, Indians, Dec. 21, 1769.*

TAYLOR, Anderson of Hollowell, and Persis Pease, Jan. 9, 1791.*

THACHER, Ladia of Lebanon, Conn., and John Deane [? Doane], June 10, ———.*

THOMAS, Tamson and Tristram Weeks, int. Apr. 5, 1845.

THOMPSON, Jone and Richard Hillman, July 3, 1775.*
Robert and Jane Nickerson, Jan. 15, 1768.*

THORP, Thomas of Edgartown, and Ruth Hillman, Mar. 17, 1768.*

TILLTON (see Tilton), Abigail and Reuben Tillton, Jan. 28, 1762.*
Allen, Capt., and Mary E. McCollum [int. McCullum, omits E.], Apr. 20, 1834.

* Intention not recorded.

CHILMARK MARRIAGES. 75

TILLTON, Asa and Sarah Smith, Mar. 19 [1801].
Bathsheba and W[illia]m Stewort, Sept. 17, 1789.*
Beriah [dup. Tilton, s. William and Abiah] and Mary Mayhew, Dec. 12, 1728.*
Bersheba and Joseas [?] Allen, Nov. 4, 1762.*
Bethiah and John Tillton, Mar. 11, 1787.*
Cathrine and Vinal Skiff, Nov. 11, 1779.*
Cornelus and Jedidah Pease, Feb. 16, 1780.*
David and Mary Tillton, July 2, 1775.*
David and Matty Skiff, Feb. 27, 1800.*
Dinah and Jese Dunham, Mar. 23, 1769.*
Dinah and Eleazer Dunham, int. Oct. 4, 1800.
Elishai and Ruth Cliffor[d], int. Feb. 22, 1804.
Elizabeth and Theophilus Mayhew, Feb. 22, 1776.*
Eunice and Oliver Tillton, [Jan.] 23, 1791.*
Ezra and Elizabeth Bassett, Oct. 28 [? 23], 1765.*
Ezra and Mary Weeks, June 20, 1779.*
Fanny and Norton Bassett Jr., Apr. 10, 1823.*
Hannah and Jonathan Tillton, Dec. 24, 1767.*
Hannah and John Flanders, Dec. 23, 1792.*
Hannah G. and Lot Besse, int. Nov. 23, 1833.
James R. and Hannah Norton, int. Apr. 26, 1834.
Jedidah and Timothy Butler, Dec. 21, 1780.*
Jemima and Silas Cottle, Mar. 19, 1795.*
Jerusha and Silas Cottle, Nov. 27, 1777.*
John and Bethiah Tillton, Mar. 11, 1787.*
Jonathan and Hannah Tillton, Dec. 24, 1767.*
Joseph Jr. and Deidamia Davis, Dec. 25, 1788.*
Josiah and Mary B. Norton, Nov. 24, 1814.*
Julia F. and Charles Vincent, int. Sept. 14, 1833.
Lucy and Reuben Hatch, Dec. 3, 1789.*
Lyda and Jethro Dunham, Apr. 10, 1776.*
Mary and David Tillton, July 2, 1775.*
Mary and Daniel Norton, June 15, 1780.*
Mary and John Gray, Feb. 17, 1789.*
Mary Jr. [dup. omits Jr.] and Robert Allen, Nov. 21, 1793.*
Matthew Jr. and Anne Robinson, int. Aug. 12, 1803.
Meribah and Jonathan Burgis, Jan. 27, 1785.*
Nancy and Willmut Mayhew, Oct. 27, 1785.*
Oliver and Eunice Tillton, [Jan.] 23, 1791.*
Olivia and William Bassett, Nov. 16, 1794.*
Pain and Susanna Tillton, Dec. 17, 1772.*
Parnal, Mrs., and Ephraim Briggs, Sept. 6, 1832.

* Intention not recorded.

CHILMARK MARRIAGES.

TILLTON, Peggy and W[illia]m Churchill 3d, —— [rec. between Apr. 14 and Apr. 21], 1791.*
Rebeccah and Stephen Tillton, Dec. 14, 1768.*
Remember and Jonathan Crowell, Apr. 14, 1791.*
Reuben and Abigail Tillton, Jan. 28, 1762.*
Ruhamah and Benjamin Smith, Aug. 22, 1793.*
Ruth and Joseph Look, Dec. 31, 1767.*
Salithiel and Unice Weeks, Nov. 18, 1781.*
Samuel and Mary Allen, May 16, 1768.*
Sidney [female] and Vincent Taber, Mar. 28, 1833.
Sophronia [int. Sophrona Tilton] and Elijah Howland, Apr. 23 [1830].
Stephen and Rebeccah Tillton, Dec. 14, 1768.*
Susanna and Pain Tillton, Dec. 17, 1772.*
Thomas and Jemima Mayhew, Dec. 9, 1725.*
Will[ia]m [dup. Tilton, s. Beriah and Mary] and Beersheba [dup. Bathsheba] Mayhew, Jan. 14, 1762.*

TILTON (see Tillton), Abiah and Timothy Mayhew, Jan. 14, 1730-1.*
Agnes L. and Capt. William Flanders, int. Jan. 25, 1840.
Alonzo and Corsandia Tilton, int. Jan. 1, 1848.
Anson of Easton, N.Y., and Julina Tilton, int. June 3, 1837.
Bathsheba and Stephen Skiff, Aug. 26, 1742.*
Benjamin S. and Susanna Hillman, Oct. 24, 1822.*
Charles and Rebecca Skiff, Nov. 22, 1840.
Charlotte [dup. and int. Tillton] and Owen Hillmar [Hillman] [dup. Hilliams] Jr., June 16 [dup. June 17], 1828.
Chatherine [dup. and int. Chatharine] M. [dup. 22], d. Elisha [and] Ruth, and Charles M. Skiff, Apr. 4, 1844.
Corsandia and Alonzo Tilton, int. Jan. 1, 1848.
Cyrano and Remember Tobey Jr., Jan. 12, 1730-1.*
David and Lavinnia Allen, Oct. 11, 1793, in Tisbury.*
David [int. Tillton] and Jedidah Robinson, Sept. 25, 1806.
Deborah M. and Nathan S. Bassett, Nov. 8, 1827.
Deidamia D. [int. 24] and George West Jr., July 31, 1842.
Ebenezar and Hepsabah Parker, Jan. 6, 1785, in Falmouth.*
Horatio W., 24, s. Josiah and Patty, and Theresa [int. Thresa] T. Bassett, Apr. 15, 1847.
Isaac and Jemima Butler, Nov. 25, 1790, in Tisbury.*
James N. and Lydia B. Norton, int. June 17, 1837.
John and Sarah Gibs, Aug. 30, 1738.*
Joseph and Zilpah Mayhew, Apr. 15, 1742.*

* Intention not recorded.

CHILMARK MARRIAGES. 77

TILTON, Josiah and Elliz[a]beth Mayhew, Feb. 23, 1743.*
Josiah [dup. Tillton] and Hannah Flanders Jr. [dup. omits Jr.], Oct. 21, 1829.
Julina and Anson Tilton, int. June 3, 1837.
Lydia S. [int. Susen, 18], d. Pain [and] Perses, and William Goff, Dec. 17, 1843.
Mary A. and Ulissus P. Luce, int. Mar. 12, 1831.
Margaret and Bartlet Norton, int. Dec. 28, 1827.
Mary A., 21, d. John and Mary, and Hiram Hammett, Sept. 28, 1845.
Mary B. and Prince D. Athearn, Nov. 29, 1838.
Matthew and Polly Dunham, Apr. 1, 1806.
Polly C. and Stephen D. Skiff, Feb. 3, 1842.
Rachel and Jonathan Lumb[e]r[t], Oct. 19, 1707.*
Salathiel and Mary Tobey, Mar. 17, 1741-2.*
Samuel and Hannah Moulton, ———, "In the year 1673 came to the Isle of Marthas Vineyard." *
Sarah and John D. Rotch, Oct. 28, 1828.
Sary Jr. [int. Sarah Tillton] and Mayhew Cottle, Dec. 13, 1804.
Shadrack R. [dup. Capt. Shaduck R., int. Capt. Shadrach R. of Tisbury], 27, s. David and Judida, and Helen [int. Hellen] M. Ferguson, Nov. 4, 1847.
Sophia and Henry W. Look, int. Mar. 8, 1848.
Thomas and Fear Hawks, May 11, 1805.
Ward and Elizabeth Chase, Nov. 3, 1784, in Tisbury.*
William, s. William and Bathsheba, and Margaret Stewart, ———.*
William, s. Samuel, and Abiah Mayhew, ———.*

TOBEY, Mary of Sandwich, and Salathiel Tilton, Mar. 17, 1741-2.*
Remember Jr. of Sandwich, and Cyrano Tilton, Jan. 12, 1730-1.*

TOCKANET (see Tauknut, Tocknet, Tockquenett), Esther and Joshua Stephens, int. Mar. 7, 1801.

TOCKNET (see Tauknut, Tockanet, Tockquenett), Hannah and Marshall Manning, int. Apr. 7, 1810.

TOCKQUENETT (see Tauknut, Tockanet, Tocknet), Elizabeth and William Weeks [Indians], ———, 1797.*
Peggy Jr. and Joseph Gershom [Indians], Aug. 22, 1796.*
Susannah and Thomas Cooper Jr. [Indians], Dec. 13, 1798.*

TRAPP, Mercy and Samuel Pease, Jan. 4, 1710.*

* Intention not recorded.

CHILMARK MARRIAGES.

TRIPP, Holder R., 21, b. New Bedford [int. of New Bedford], s. Francis and Any A. of New Bedford, and Mary D. Hayden, Jan. 1, 1846.

TUFS, Elizabeth and Ichobud Hach, May 18, 1781.*

TURNER, Japhet and Eliza[be]th Hillman, Apr. 21, 1763.*

VINCENT (see Vinson), Charles of Edgartown, and Julia F. Tillton, int. Sept. 14, 1833.
Herman and Louisa Mayhew, Nov. 6, 1831.
Moses C., 24, b. Tisbury, s. William S. [and] Hannah of Tisbury, and Harriet N. Hillman, Mar. 20, 1846.

VINSON (see Vincent), Abiah of Edgartown, and Simon Mayhew, Apr. 27, 1749.*
Joseph of Edgartown, and Thankful Stuart, July 10, 1766.*
Matilda and Simon Mayhew, Apr. 21, 1796.*

WADSWORTH, Bethyah and Zephaniah Mayhew, Mar. —, 1711.*
Polite of Kingston, and Zephaniah Mayhew, Nov. 24, 1773, in Tisbury.*

WAINIER, Paul of Westport, Bristol Co., and Cloe Cuff, int. Sept. 29, 1804.

WALDRON (see Warldred), Will[ia]m and Elizabeth [dup. Elizebeth] Allen, Dec. 28, 1721.*

WAMSLAY (see Wamsley, Warmsley, Womsley, Woormsly, Wormsley), Harriet A. of Gayhead, and Isaac A. Rose, int. Apr. 5, 1841.

WAMSLEY (see Wamslay, Warmsley, Womsley, Woormsly, Wormsley), Hebron Jr. of Gayhead, and Ele [?] Peters, int. May 23, 1840.
Hebron of Gayhead, and Jane Francies, int. Aug. 14, 1846.

WARD, Peggy and Isaac Johnson Jr., Jan. 29, 1798.*

WARLDRED (see Waldron), Margaret and Nathan Skiff, Mar. 13, 1766.*

WARMSLEY (see Wamslay, Wamsley, Womsley, Woormsly, Wormsley), Elizabeth of Gayhead, and Zaccheus Hourvoiwee, int. Aug. 21, 1827.

* Intention not recorded.

CHILMARK MARRIAGES.

WASS, Margate and Pain Mayhew Jr., Nov. 17, 1757.*

WEEKS, Abegail and Ichabod Hatch, Sept. 2, 1714, in Falmouth.*
Elizabeth and Bryant Cartwright, Oct. 19, 1732.*
Eunice (see Unice).
Expereance of Falmouth, and William Cockran, Nov. 1, 1758, in Falmouth.*
Hannah B. and John W. Gifford, int. Nov. 24, 1840.
Lemuel of Falmouth, and Deliverance Palmer, Dec. 29, 1746, in Falmouth.*
Mary and Nathan Hatch, Sept. 2, 1714, in Falmouth.*
Mary and Ezra Tillton, June 20, 1779.*
Mehitable and Ichabod Johnson, Nov. 26, 1718, in Falmouth.*
Nabby of Falmouth, Barnstable Co., and Paul Robinson, int. Oct. 5, 1804.
Nathan and Remember Laurence, Aug. 10, 1737, in Falmouth.*
Rebecca and Samuel Robinson, Aug. 4, 1780, in Falmouth.*
Shubil and Mercy Prince, Feb. 7, 1710.*
Soloman of Tisbury, and Lydia Horton, int. Oct. 2, 1802.
Tamer and John Nye, Feb. 9, 1774.*
Tristram of Gayhead, and Mrs. Peggey F. Jonas, int. June 17, 1843.
Tristram and Tamson Thomas, int. Apr. 5, 1845.
Unice and Salithiel Tillton, Nov. 18, 1781.*
William and Elizabeth Tockquenett [Indians], ———, 1797.*

WEST, George Jr. [int. 25] and Deidamia D. Tilton, July 31, 1842.
Leonard and Rebecca Flanders, May 5, 1826.*
Lovey and Vincent Taber, int. Apr. 7, 1827.
Lydia and Richard Fisher, Nov. 9, 1799.*
Lydia and Thomas H. Lumbut, Jan. 22, 1825.*
Mary and John Cottle, Dec. 3, 1717.*
Moses L. and Rebecca W. West, int. Aug. 8, 1835.
Prudence and William Mitchel, int. Feb. 2, 1833.
Rebecca W. and Moses L. West, int. Aug. 8, 1835.
Salley and Warren Luce, Oct. 19, 1797.*
Thomas of Tisbury, and Sarah Butler, Dec. 21, 1775.*
William of Tisbury, and Mary Poole, int. Nov. 12, 1808.
William C. and Abby A. Luce, int. May 19, 1849.

WHITE, Abraham [int. adds C.] of West Port [int. Westport], and Nancy A. Gifford, Sept. 11, 1833.

* Intention not recorded.

CHILMARK MARRIAGES.

WHITE, Matild of New Bedford, and Benjamin Pearse, int. May 11, 1847.
Sarah and Benja[mi]n Luce, Aug. 25, 1774.*
WILLIAMS, Anna of Sandwich, and Rev. Jonathan Smith, Oct. 25, 1789.*
Anna [int. Anny] B. and William Cottle, Jan. 23, 1806.
Caroline and John Cottle Jr., int. Mar. 5, 1809.
WILTSIC, John R., widr. [int. omits widr.], 30, of Newburg [int. Newburgh], N.Y., and Mary S. Spofford, Jan. 9, 1845.
WIMPENNEY, William and Hannah Clark, Feb. 26, 1746.*
WINSLOW, Isaac of Tisbury, and Deborah Lumbert, Nov. 20 [1800].
James, 19, s. Peleg and Rebecca, and Hulda [int. Huldah] R. Gifford, Nov. 14, 1844.
WOMSLEY (see Wamslay, Wamsley, Warmsley, Woormsly, Wormsley), Priscilla of Gayhead, and Isaac Rows, int. May 23, 1837.
WOORMSLY (see Wamslay, Wamsley, Warmsley, Womsley, Wormsley), Hebron and Amy P. Awker, int. Apr. 1, 1809.
WORMSLEY (see Wamslay, Wamsley, Warmsley, Womsley, Woormsly), Jane, Mrs. [int. of Gayhead], and Thomas Cooper, May 7, 1837.
WORTH, Will[ia]m of Edgartown, and Mary Butler, Oct. 24, 1717.*
William, Capt., of Edgartown, and Martha Allen, Apr. 5, 1788.*

UNIDENTIFIED.

———, Catharine and Abishai Cottle, Nov. 3, 1765.*
———, Deborah A. and Thomas H. Lumbut, Nov. 26, 1817.*
[Thomas H. Lambert, Nov. 26, 1818, G.R.]
———, Mary and Matthew Mayhew, Mar. 1, 1674.*

* Intention not recorded.

CHILMARK DEATHS.

CHILMARK DEATHS.

To the year 1850.

ADAMS, David B., dropsy, June —, 1841, a. 13 m. [s. David and Phebe, June 12, a. 1 y. 21 d., G.R.]
Elishib, ch. Capt. Mayhew and Rebeccah, Nov. 15, 1771.
Mayhew, Capt. [h. Rebecca], Sept. 10, 1823, a. 96. G.R.
Moses, Capt., typhoid pneumonia, Apr. 13, 1843, a. 30 y. 4 m. 15 d. [[h. Martha] Apr. 17, a. 80 y. 4 m., G.R.]
Phebe M., d. David and Phebe, Nov. 28, 1832, a. 13 m. 20 d. G.R.
Rebecca, w. Capt. Mayhew, July 11, 1819, a. 89. G.R.
Reliance, w. Eliashit, Jan. 8, 1729-30, in 34th y. G.R.
Susan W., Mrs., chlorosis, Dec. 13 [1842], a. 23 y. 3 m. 19 d. [w. Moses, Dec. 12, G.R.]
———, s. Calvin C. and Lydia, still born, Sept. 4, 1846.

ALLEN, Abigail [ch. John and Margaret], Aug. 12, 1726.
Abigail, wid., July 12, 1806.
Abigal [ch. Eben[ezer] and Rebeckah], July 31, 1710.
Ann, wid. John, June 3, 1794. [— 4, 1795, G.R.]
Anthony, s. Capt. James, June 29, 1777, in 32d y., in captivity, in N.Y. G.R.
Bathsheba, w. Josiah, Feb. 20, 1825, a. 79 y. 10 m. G.R.
Beulah, May 28, 1806.
Beulah, w. Dea. Ezra, Oct. 26, 1830, a. 69 y. 9 [8, written above in pencil] m.
Catharine, w. Silvanus, Sept. 15, 1827, a. 54. G.R.
Clarissa, dysentery, Aug. —, 1841, a. 71. [w. Tristram, Aug. 26, a. 70, G.R.]
Deborah, w. Jonathan, Apr. 19, 1821. [wid. Jonathan Esq., in 78th y., G.R.]
Deborah, d. Tristram, Dec. 11, 1847, a. 40. G.R.
Deborah, ——— [rec. between June 19, 1847, and Jan. 29, 1848].
Desire, w. Robert, June 13, 1792. [in 61st y., G.R.]
Ebenezer Esq., May 14, 1783, in 62d y. G.R.

ALLEN, Eleazer Esq., Nov. 7, 1735, in 30th y. G.R.
Eleaz[e]r, ch. John and Margaret, Oct. 2, 1740.
Elizabeth, d. John and Margaret, Mar. 20, 1790.
Ezra, Dea. [h. Beulah], Mar. 30, 1833, a. 77 y. 8 m., in New York City. G.R.
Frederick, s. Henry, ——, 1806. [s. Henry and Sophia, Jan. 2, a. 1 y. 10 m., G.R.]
Hannah, ch. John and Margaret, Aug. 30, 1741.
James [h. Mary], Feb. 14, 1723-4, a. abt. 50. G.R.
James, Capt., Jan. 7, 1786, in 70th y. G.R.
James, s. Ebenezer and Rebecah, Jan. 14, 1786.
James, Dea. [h. Martha], Nov. 3, 1815, a. 84. G.R.
Jane, w. Silvanus, Dec. —, 1763. [Dec. 17, in 63d y., G.R.]
Jane, d. John and Margaret, Apr. 5, 1775.
John, s. John and Margaret [dup. [h. Ann]], Oct. 8, 1756.
John Esq. [h. Margaret], Oct. 17, 1767. [Col. John Esq., Oct. 7, in 83d y., G.R.]
Jonathan [dup. Esq.], s. John and Margaret [dup. [h. Deborah]], Jan. 6, 1784. [in 50th y., G.R.]
Josiah [h. Bathsheba], Aug. 11, 1821, in 83d y. G.R.
Katherine, [twin] d. John and Margaret, June 6, 1741.
Love, June 13, 1787.
Margaret, d. John and Margaret, Sept. 1, 1745.
Margaret, d. John and Ann, Apr. 7, 1754, a. 2 m. 1 d. G.R.
Margaret, w. John Esq., Apr. 26, 1778. [w. Col. John, in 83d y., G.R.]
Margarett C., ch. Ephrain and Rebecca, Sept. 27, 1827. [Margaret C., a. 11, G.R.]
Martha, w. Dea. James, Oct. 26, 1826, a. 93. G.R.
Mary, w. James, May 20, 1722, a. 44. G.R.
Mary, w. Samuel, Dec. 25, 1756.
Mary, d. John and Margaret, July 2, 1783.
Nathan, ——, 1733, in 21st y. G.R.
Patience, w. Matthew, Nov. 6, 1797, a. 20. G.R.
Peggy, ch. John and Ann, Apr. 7, 1754.
Pelnrah, d. Josiah and Bathsheba, consumption, Apr. 7, 1847, a. 73.
Rebeckah, d. John and Margaret, May 29, 1790.
Robert [h. Desire], Jan. 10, 1801, in 69th y. G.R.
Samuel [h. Mary], July 12, 1755. [a. 78, G.R.]
Samuel, ch. Ephraim and Hannah, Apr. 27, 1783.
Sarah, Jan. 23, 1812, a. 18. G.R.
Silvanus [h. Jane], Oct. 9, 1787. [in 86th y., G.R.]

ALLEN, Theodore, s. Jonathan and Deborah, Aug. 27, 1768. [s. Jonathan Esq. and Deborah, a. 1 y. 5 m., G.R.]
Tristram, s. Jonathan and Deborah, Aug. 10, 1768. [s. Jonathan Esq. and Deborah, a. 3 y. 5 m., G.R.]
William, s. John and Margaret, June 2, 1746. [in 27th y., G.R.]
William, s. Silvanus and Jane, Oct. 20, 1752, a. 18. G.R.
William, ch. Silvanus and Jane, Oct. 28, 1753.
————, s. Matthew W. and Mary Ann, still [born], Aug. 20, 1845.

BASSETT (see Bassitt), Anna, w. William, Sept. 25, 1780, in 71st y. G.R.
Baraciah, ch. Nathan and Mary, Oct. 3, 1728.
Cornelius, Col., Oct. 1, 1778, in 56th y. G.R.
Cornelus, ch. Nathan and Mary, drounded, Jan. 12, 1714.
Elizabath, d. John and Jean, Aug. 10, 1776.
Elizabeth, ch. Nathan and Mary, ————.
Hope, ch. Nathan and Mary, Feb. 17, 1761.
Jane, w. John, Apr. 19, 1803, a. 88 y. 7 m. G.R.
John, ch. Nathan and Mary, July 12, 1791. [[h. Jane] a. 85 y. 2 m. 26 d., G.R.]
Katharine, w. Nathaniel, Mar. 7, 1798.
Martha, w. Nathan [*sic*, in pencil], Nov. 2, 1790, in 35th y. G.R.
Mary, w. Nathan, Nov. 8, 1743, in 71st y. G.R.
Mary, ch. Nathan and Mary, Mar. 8, 1785.
Nathan, ch. Nathan and Mary, June 26, 1730.
Nathan [h. Mary], Nov. 16, 1743, in 77th y. G.R.
Nathan S., s. Nathan S. and Deborah, Nov. 26, 1840, a. 18 m. G.R.
Nathaniel, ch. Nathan and Mary, Aug. 11, 1715.
Nathaniel Esq., Mar. 13, 1804, in 77th y. G.R.
Norton [h. Fanny], Nov. 7, 1836. G.R.
Ruth, ch. Nathan and Mary, Dec. —, 1691.
Samuel, ch. Nathan and Mary, Nov. 20, 1770.
William, ch. Nathan and Mary, Dec. 24, 1782. [[h. Anna] in 80th y., G.R.]
Ziphorah, d. Benjamin Esq. and Abigail, Mar. 16, 1812. G.R.
————, s. Norton Jr. and Fanny, ———— [? Feb. 22, 1824].

BASSITT (see Bassett), Abigail, ch. Benjamin and Abigail, Oct. 26, 1808. [Bassett, G.R.]

BOARDMAN, Andrew, Rev., Nov. 19, 1776. [Rev. Andrew, A.M., a. 56, G.R.]

BOSWORTH, Elizabeth, w. Belomy, June 9, 1747, in 30th y.
G.R.

BURGIS, Benjamin, Feb. 10, 1752, a. 39. G.R.

CHASE, Joseph, Capt., May 20, 1832, a. 49 y. 4 m. 21 d. G.R.

CLAGHORN, Experience, w. Shubael, Sept. 19, 1778, in 72d y.
G.R.
Shubael [h. Experience], Jan. 14, 1754, in 54th y. G.R.

CLARK, Bethiah, w. W[illia]m, Feb. 22, 1735, in 44th y. [in 49th y., G.R.]
William, Capt., Mar. 6, 1827, a. 62. G.R.

COTTEN, Mary [w. Miles], Feb. 18, 1787.

COTTLE, Mary Ann, w. Truman, d. Tristram Allen and Clarissa, canker rash and scarlet fever, May 10, 1847, a. 45 y. 3 m. 29 d.
Mary E., d. Mayhew and Sally, Sept. 12, 1828, a. 11 m. G.R.
Silas [h. Jamima], Aug. —, 1824, a. 72. G.R.

COTTON (see Cotten).

CRANE, Judith, decay of nature, Nov. — [1841], a. 96.

DAVIS, Mary Ann, b. Stonington, Conn., w. John, d. ———
Bemet [Bennet], cancer, Mar. 20 [30], 1846, a. 42 y. 3 m. 15 d.
Sophronia, disease of the heart, Jan. — [1842], a. 43.
———, d. John and Mary Ann, still [born], June 2, 1845.

DUNHAM, ———, d. John and Nancy, still [born], Apr. 28, 1846.

FLANDERS, Abby Jane, dysentery, Aug. 9, 1842, a. 2 y. 2 m. 6 d. [Abba Jane, ch. Daniel and Charlotte, G.R.]
Agnes, d. William and Agnes, dropsy in the brain, Apr. 10, 1845, a. 7 m. 14 d.
Agnes L., b. Nantucket, w. William, d. Beriah Tilton and Julia, pulmonary consumption, June 24, 1845, a. 24 y. 6 m. 29 d. [Agnes, a. 25, G.R.]
Charlott, Mrs., dysentery, Aug. 21 [1842], a. 32 y. 10 m. 17 d. [Charlotte, w. Daniel, Aug. 25, a. 32 y. 10 m., G.R.]
Charlotte, ch. Daniel and Charlotte, Jan. 3, 1837. G.R.
Charlotte, w. Daniel, Aug. 25, 1842, a. 32 y. 10 m. G.R.
Clarissa, d. Alvin and Maribah, consumption, June 19, 1846, a. 20 y. 4 m. 30 d. [Clarissa G., d. Alvin and Meribah, Jan. 14, 1845, a. 19, G.R.]

FLANDERS, Daniel T., ch. Alvin and Meribah, July 6, 1837,
a. 1 y. 2 m. G.R.
John [h. Hannah], Apr. 25, 1837, a. 67. G.R.
Joseph, ch. Alvin [and] Meribah, concumption, Jan. 11, 1844,
a. 4 y. 4 m. 29 d. [Jan. 14, 1845, a. 4 y. 5 m., G.R.]

FOLGER, Sarah, "formerly Mayhew," July 11, 1734.

GRINNELL, Hannah, wid., b. Middleborough, d. Paul Dean
and Rebecca, lung fever, Apr. 12, 1846, a. 72 y. 2 m. 11 d.

HAMMETT, Gilbert, fever, July 24, 1841, a. 17, at sea.

HANCOCK, James, s. John and Mary, lost at sea, Nov. 9, 1811,
a. 18 y. 5 d. G.R.
John Esq. [h. Mary], June 23, 1841, a. 72. G.R.
John Esq., cancer of the stomach, July —, 1841, a. 71.
Rodney, s. John and Mary, Mar. 17, 1822, a. 17 y. 11 m. 7 d.
G.R.
Rodolphus, s. John and Mary, Sept. 30, 1838, a. 32. G.R.

HILLMAN, James, s. James and Dinah, Aug. 20, 1798, a. 19.
G.R.
James, Aug. 9, 1819, a. 38. G.R.
Maria, puerperal fever of the brain, May 8, 1841, a. 38. [w.
Isaiah, a. 39 y. 4 m. 25 d., G.R.]
Owen, Capt. [h. Polly], Apr. 13, 1835, a. 70 y. 4 m. 9 d. G.R.
Pardon, [Oct.] 29, 1807.
Phebe, "town pauper," July 20, 1829, a. 100 y. 2 m. 16 d.
Polly, wid. Capt. Owen, Feb. 1, 1840, a. 65. G.R.
Rebecca, w. Capt. Robert, Oct. 31, 1815, a. 70 y. 3 m. 11 d.
G.R.
Robert, Capt. [h. Rebecca], Oct. 20, 1824. G.R.
Samuel, Jan. 27, 1801, in 69th y. G.R.
Stephen, May 9, 1826, a. 57. G.R.
Susanna, w. Silas, Oct. 26, 1834, in 55th y. G.R.
Zerviah, decay of nature, Feb. —, 1842, a. 94.
———, s. Owen Jr. and Charlotte, Nov. 3, 1832.
———, d. Owen Jr. and Charlotte, Feb. 12, 1836.

HOLMES (see Homes), Katherine, wid. William, Apr. 10, 1754,
in 82d y. G.R.

HOMES (see Holmes), John, Oct. 14, 1732, a. 32. G.R.
William, Rev. [h. Katherine], June 27, 1746, in 84th y. G.R.

HOWLAND, Charles Otis, ch. Elijah [and] Sophronia, tippas fever, Aug. 25, 1843, a. 3 y. 5 m. 13 d.

HUNT, Hannah, w. William, "formerly" w. Lt. Benjamin Mayhew, Jan. 25, 1747, in 63d y. G.R.

Jane, w. William, Oct. 19, 1732, in 56th y. G.R.

Sarah, Mrs., Oct. 16, 1770, in 94th y., "formerly the wife of Mr. Samuel Bradford of Plympton, Gentleman and who deceased March 26. 1740 in the 56th year of his age, who left eight children: names as follows, John, Gideon, Mary, Sarah, William, Abigail Phebe and Samuel . . . who was the daughter of Mr. Edward Gray and Mary his wife of Tiverton. Born April 8th. 1697." G.R.

William Sr. [h. Jane], Jan. 2, 1727, a. abt. 73. G.R.

JONES, Daniel [h. Mary], June 20, 1816, a. 76 y. 3 m. 15 d. G.R.

Daniel, s. Daniel and Polly, May 1, 1847, a. 64 y. 6 m. 11 d. [a. 64 y. 6 m. 4 d., G.R.]

Mary, wid. Daniel, Mar. 1, 1825, a. 74 y. 6 m. 17 d. G.R.

Thomas, Oct. 22, 1826, a. 41 y. 1 m. 17 d., in New Bedford. G.R.

LAMBERT (see Lumbert), Abishai H., Apr. 13, 1827, a. 57. G.R.

John, lost at sea, Jan. 24, 1824. G.R.

Moses, Aug. 3, 1819, a. 81 y. 8 m. 8 d. G.R.

Nancy, [twin] ch. ———, July 30, 1834, a. 59 y. 5 m. 22 d. G.R.

Peggy, [twin] ch. ———, Apr. 9, 1840, a. 65 y. 2 m. 1 d. G.R.

Sarah, Mar. 26, 1828, a. 88 y. 5 m. 11 d. G.R.

Thomas, Feb. 11, 1815, a. 47 y. 6 m. G.R.

LITTLE, Jedidah [w. Tho[ma]s], Aug. 19, 1731. [w. Dr. Thomas, in 27th y., G.R.]

LOOK, Eliza, wid. Allen, Aug. 18, 1847, a. 53. G.R.

Lovina, d. George and Perses, July 27, 1826, a. 13 y. 10 m. 4 d. G.R.

Prince Jr., June 15, 1821, a. 24 y. 8 m. 5 d. G.R.

Prince, b. Tisbury, ch. Job [and] Martha, cancer in the face, July 16, 1843, a. 90 y. 6 m. [[h. Sarah] a. 93 y. 2 m. 6 d., G.R.]

Reuben, Jan. 20, 1827, a. 38 y. 5 d. G.R.

Sarah, w. Prince, Apr. 18, 1800, a. 36. G.R.

LUCE, ———, b. Tisbury, d. Charles and Catharine, whooping cough, July 1, 1846, a. 2 m.

LUMBERT (see Lambert), Deborah A. [w. Thomas H. (Lumbut)], May 31, 1818. [Lambert, May 31, 1819, a. 18 y. 4 m., G.R.]
James, ch. Moses (Lumbart) and Sarah, Oct. 26, 1766.
Laura H., dysentery and typhoid fever, Sept. 4 [1842], a. 7 y. 4 m. 6 d. [Laura G. Lambert, d. Hon. Thomas H. and Lydia W., Sept. 5, a. 7 y. 4 m., G.R.]

MANTOR, ———, ch. Sam[ue]l, Oct. 20, 1806.

MAYHEW, Abiah, w. Simon, Nov. 3, 1792, in 64th y. G.R.
Abner [h. Martha], Oct. 21, 1830, a. 80 y. 8 m. 25 d. G.R.
Adonijah [ch. Zephaniah and Bethiah], Mar. 19, 1714.
Allen, s. Matthew and Mary, Dec. 9, 1826. [Dr. Allen [h. Eunice], a. 50, G.R.]
Anna, old age, Mar. 8, 1845, a. 84 y. 11 m. 12 d. [a. 85, G.R.]
Benjamin, Lt., Aug. 30, 1717. [Benjamin, Aug. 31, in 39th y., G.R.]
Benjamin Esq. [h. Lydia], Aug. 11, 1826, a. 82 y. 3 m. 3 d. G.R.
Bethiah, w. Zepheniah, Jan. 19, 1767, in 80th y.
Clarissa, w. George, Nov. 3, 1829, a. 32. G.R.
David, Sept. 24, 1821, a. 42. G.R.
Elizabeth, w. Zachariah, Mar. 20, 1790. [w. Rev. Zechariah, in 70th y., G.R.]
Elizabeth, wid. Theophilus, d. Josiah Tilton [and] Eliziabeth, old age, Feb. 18, 1844, a. 85 y. 6 m. 11 d. [Feb. 17, 1845, a. 87, G.R.]
Elizabeth A., July 4, 1830, a. 11. G.R.
Ephraim, Oct. 4, 1807. [[h. Jedidah], in 62d y., G.R.]
Eunice, w. Dr. Allen, Oct. 17, 1841, a. 69. G.R.
Experance, Mr., Nov. 29, 1758. [Rev. Experience, A.M., apoplexy, G.R.]
Gideon, old age, Jan. — [? 1849], a. 70.
Hannah, d. Pain and Mary, June 7, 1715.
Hannah G., w. John, Dec. 17, 1801, in 35th y. G.R.
Harriet, Sept. 29, 1806. [d. Thomas and Parnel, a. 19 y. 1 m. 16 d., G.R.]
Hillyard, ch. Ephraim and Jedidah, Aug. 7, 1817. [Hilliard, apoplex, in 27th y., G.R.]
James, s. Nathan and Susanah, Aug. 20, 1783.
Jane, ch. Simon [and] Abiah, Aug. 28, 1768.
Jane, wid. Dea. Oliver, Jan. 24, 1833, a. 68 y. 9 m. 7 d. G.R.
Jane, liver complaint, Apr. — [? 1849], a. 72.
Jedidah, w. Ephraim, May 11, 1826, a. 74. G.R.

CHILMARK DEATHS.

MAYHEW, Jerusha, d. Zephaniah and Bethiah, Feb. 22, 1793.
Jethro, Oct. 16, 1806. [in 65th y., G.R.]
John, Mar. 3, 1736, a. abt. 60. G.R.
John [h. Hannah G.], Apr. 19, 1827, a. 74 y. 10 m. G.R.
Jonathan [h. Parnel], Dec. 7, 1805, in 52d y. G.R.
Jonathan, Rev., Aug. 26, 1826, a. 29. G.R.
Joseph, Feb. 7, 1779. G.R.
Julia, d. Rev. Jonathan, Aug. 5, 1825, a. 2 y. 10 m. G.R.
Lois, w. Capt. Samuel, May 8, 1802, in 84th y. G.R.
Lydia, old age, Aug. — [? 1848].
Lydia, w. Benjamin Esq., Sept. 2, 1848, a. 83 y. 10 m. 18 d. G.R.
Lydia R., d. Timothy and Ruth, dysentary, Oct. 15, 1849, a. 68.
Martha, d. Pain and Mary, Jan. 22, 1750.
Martha, d. M[atthe]w and Mary, May 31, 1775. [in 24th y., G.R.]
Martha, d. Thomas and Parnel, July 15, 1806, a. 17 y. 2 m. 8 d. G.R.
Martha, w. Abner, Mar. 20, 1821, in 71st y. G.R.
Mary, w. Pain, Feb. 17, 1753 "N. S.," a. 77.
Mary, w. Matthew, July 2, 1783. [w. Matthew Esq., in 56th y., G.R.]
Matthew, Dr. [h. Mary], Aug. 10, 1805, in 85th y. G.R.
Matthew Esq. [h. Rebecca], July 6, 1838, a. abt. 83, in Edgartown. G.R.
Mercy, w. Seth, Sept. 12, 1800, a. 59 y. 5 m. 3 d. G.R.
Nathan, ch. Zachariah and Elizabeth, Mar. 15, 1791. [Dea. Nathan [h. Susannah], in 50th y., G.R.]
Nathan, Capt., epilipsy, July 26, 1800, in 35th y. G.R.
Oliver, Dea. [h. Jane], Aug. 25, 1828, a. 65 y. 2 m. 18 d. G.R.
Pain Jr. [ch. Pain and Mary], July 11, 1731.
Pain Esq., May 8, 1761, in 84th y. G.R.
Parnel, wid. Jonathan, Feb. 10, 1808, a. 47. G.R.
Parnel, w. Thomas, Mar. 23, 1812, in 55th y. G.R.
Patty, July 15, 1806.
Peggy, w. Jeremiah, "formerly" w. W[illia]m, Sept. 21, 1795. [second w. Capt. Jeremiah of New Bedford, in 48th y., G.R.]
Rebecca, w. Matthew Esq., suddenly, Dec. 17, 1824, a. 68. G.R.
Rebeckah, w. Zach[eu]s, Nov. 22, 1767. [w. Zacheus Esq., fourth d. Capt. Lemuel Pope of Dartmouth, a. 40 "wanting 6 days," G.R.]

MAYHEW, Rebekah, ch. Zachariah and Elizabeth, May 13, 1786. [Rebecca, youngest d. Rev. Zechariah and Elizabeth, a. 20 y. 5 m. 7 d., G.R.]
Remember, w. Experience, Mar. 2, 1722, in 39th y. G.R.
Rufus Warren, s. Hariph and Sally, Feb. 9, 1843, a. 8 m. 8 d. G.R.
Ruhamah, old age, Mar. 10 [? 1849], a. 94.
Sally, w. Mayhew, Nov. 17, 1827, a. 42 y. 8 m. 3 d. G.R.
Samuel, Capt. [h. Lois], Apr. 8, 1800, in 89th y. G.R.
Seth [h. Mercy], Sept. 20, 1800, a. 60 y. 5 m. 5 d. G.R.
Simon, Dea., Mar. 5, 1753, a. 66 y. 7 m. 10 d. G.R.
Simon, Dea., eldest ch. Dea. Simon, "was sixteen years a preacher of the gospel and at the time of his death Chief Justice in the County of Dukes," Mar. 31, 1782, a. 73 y. 22 d. G.R.
Simon [h. Abiah], June 19, 1801, in 82d y. G.R.
Simon, m., s. Simon and Abiah, old age, Mar. 31, 1847, a. 93 y. 4 m. 16 d. [[h. Matilda] G.R.]
Sophronia, d. Ephraim and Susan, Aug. 9, 1828, a. 13 y. 2 m. 26 d. G.R.
Susan, d. Matthew and Rebecca, Aug. 13, 1837, a. 54. G.R.
Susan Pease, d. Ephraim and Susan, Apr. 1, 1834, a. 23 y. 11 m. 15 d. G.R.
Susannah, w. Col. Zacheus, May 23, 1758, in 67th y. G.R.
Susannah, w. Nathan, Dec. 30, 1778. [d. Jethro Athearn of Tisbury, in 43d y., G.R.]
Theophilus, Apr. 25, 1752, a. 49. G.R.
Theophilus, Aug. 7, 1829, a. 77. G.R.
Thomas, Oct. 20, 1759 "N. S.," in 50th y.
Thomas [h. Parnel], June 4, 1808, in 52d y. G.R.
Timothy, s. Timothy and Ruth, apoplexy, Dec. 18, 1845, a. 62 y. 2 m. 17 d. [Dec. 18, 1846, G.R.]
Tristram, ch. Ephraim and Jedidah, Aug. —, 1810. [in 24th y., in London, Eng., G.R.]
William, ch. Ephraim and Jedidah, ———.
William Esq. [h. Peggy], July 13, 1785.
William B. [h. Prudence A.], Nov. 4, 1825, a. 47. G.R.
Zachariah, Rev., Mar. 6, 1806. [Rev. Zechariah [h. Elizabeth], in 88th y., G.R.]
Zacheus, Col. [h. Rebeckah], Jan. 3, 1760, in 76th y. G.R.
Zacheus Esq., July 11, 1775. [in 53d y., G.R.]
Zadoc, s. Geo[rge] and Clarissa, July 11, 1829, a. 6 m. G.R.
Zephaniah, ch. Zephaniah and Hannah, Nov. 19, 1737.
Zephaniah 1st [dup. omits 1st], ch. Zephaniah and Hannah, Oct. 27, 1749.

MAYHEW, Zepheniah, Nov. 20, 1733, in 47th y. [Zephaniah, G.R.]
———, inf. s. Benjamin and Lydia, Mar. 19, 1809. G.R.

McCOLLUM, Archibald, Sept. 3, 1840, a. 65. G.R.

NICKERSON, Albert, ch. Joseph and Eliza P., Feb. 23, 1842, a. 7 m. 20 d. G.R.
Jane, w. Capt. Samuel, Oct. 8, 1815, a. 50 y. 3 m. G.R.
Samuel, Capt. [h. Jane], Oct. 31, 1822, a. 65 y. 3 m. 20 d. G.R.
Samuel, s. Samuel and Clarissa, Nov. 6, 1840, a. 14 m. G.R.
Thomas, ch. Samuel and Clarrissa, Oct. 15, 1836, a. 13 m. 23 d. [s. Samuel and Clarissa, a. 14 m., G.R.]

NORTON, Baze, Capt., "drowned near Gay Head," Jan. 14, 1782, a. 36. G.R.
Betsy, Sept. 2, 1848. G.R.
Clement Bassett, ch. William and Polly, Feb. 6, 1796.
Clement Bassett, ch. William and Polly, Apr. 15 [? 13], 1797.
Constant, Oct. —, 1756, in 20th y.
Elizabeth, w. Capt. Samuel, Sept. 6, 1791, in 42d y. G.R.
Jacob, Jan. 4, 1750.
Jacob, drowned, Apr. 12, 1793, a. 53 y. 28 d. G.R.
James [h. Rebekah], Aug. 5, 1780, in 74th y. G.R.
Mary B., wid. Tristram, May 15, 1842, a. 82 y. 7 m. 21 d. G.R.
Peter, Oct. 10, 1759.
Peter, Oct. 15, 1759, in 18th y.
Rebecca, June 28, 1839, a. 65 y. 4 m. 20 d.
Rebekah, wid. James, Apr. 8, 1805, in 87th y. G.R.
Samuel Esq., Feb. 16, 1760, in 87th y. G.R.
Samuel, m., s. Samuel and Elizabeth, gravel and effection of the kidnys, Jan. 29, 1848, a. 64 y. 4 m. 24 d. [a. 65, G.R.]
Shobal, Feb. 15, 1760, in 27th y.
William, Feb. 28, 1802.
———, [twin] s. Samuel and Eunice, ——— [? Aug. 3, 1816].
———, [twin] s. Samuel and Eunice, ——— [? Aug. 3, 1816].

PEASE, Eliza, d. Nathaniel and Eliza, Sept. 7, 1796, a. 1 m. G.R.
Hannah, Mrs., decay of nature, diarrhea and dysentery, Aug. 12 [1842], a. 39 y. 3 m. 2 d. [w. Capt. John, a. 89 y. 3 m. 2 d., G.R.]
John [h. Hannah], June 10, 1831, a. 85 y. 4 m. G.R.
John Jr., Jan. 25, 1841, a. 53 y. 7 m. 3 d. G.R.
John, Aug. 20, 1847, in 27th y. G.R.

CHILMARK DEATHS.

PEASE, Martha, d. Capt. John and Hannah, July 7, 1833, a 4 y. 7 d. G.R.
Polly, Nov. —, 1806.

POOLE, Mary, w. Ephraim, Aug. 30, 1806. [in 27th y., G.R.]

REED, Lemuel, typhus fever, Sept. — [? 1848], a. 25. [Lemuel B., Sept. 23, 1848, G.R.]

ROBINSON, Shadrach, decay of nature, Apr. — [1842], a. 34. [[h. Deborah] Apr. 6, 1841, a. 84 y. 2 m. 4 d., G.R.]

SCOTT, William, "a native of Ireland, Londonderry Co. parish of Cumber," Nov. 6, 1833. G.R.

SKIFF (see Skiffe), Abigail, w. Benjamin, Mar. 4, 1738-9, in 37th y. G.R.
Bathsheda, dropsy and delirium, Jan. — [1842]. [Bathsheba, w. Stephen Esq., Jan. 5, in 50th y., G.R.]
Bethsheba, w. Stephen, Nov. 3, 1767.
Caleb, Apr. 10, 1769, in 27th y. G.R.
Catharine (see Catharine Smith).
Deborah, w. Ebenezer Esq., Mar. 15, 1826, a. 69 y. 10 m. G.R.
Ebenezer Esq. [h. Deborah], June 30, 1834, a. 83 y. 6 m. G.R.
Frederick Bolton, s. Stephen and Bathsheba, Nov. 26, 1837, in 27th y., at sea. G.R.
Joanna (see Joanna Smith).
Joseph [h. Remember], Nov. 7, 1778, a. 71. G.R.
Lydia, Nov. 8, 1748. [wid. James, in 63d y., G.R.]
Polly C., w. Stephen D., d. Elisha Tilton [and] Ruth, disease of the heart, Oct. 16, 1843, a. 25 y. 4 m. 4 d.
Remember, wid. Joseph, May 21, 1815, a. 100 y. 8 m. 21 d. G.R.
Sarah, d. John Tillton and Sarah, Dec. 23, 1762. [w. Nathan, "formerly" w. Theophilus Mayhew, "formerly" w. Benjamin Mayhew, in 46th y., G.R.]
Vinal [h. Catharine], Apr. 19, 1829, a. 70 y. 2 m. 9 d. G.R.
———, s. Samuel E. and Eunice M., premature birth, June 19, 1847, a. 7½ hrs.

SKIFFE (see Skiff), Benjamin Esq. [h. Hannah], Feb. 17, 1717-18, a. 62. G.R.
Hannah, w. Benjamin Esq., Feb. 27, 1758, in 98th y. G.R.
James, June 6, 1724. [Skiff [h. Lydia], G.R.]
John, Mar. 6, 1728, a. 22. G.R.

SKIFFE, Mercy, w. Nathan, June 12, 1724, a. 56. G.R.
Nathan [h. Mercy], Feb. 12, 1725–6, a. 71. G.R.

SMITH, Abigail, w. Shobal, June 7, 1718, a. 53. G.R.
Anna, w. Rev. Jonathan, [Oct.] 26, 1807. [in 49th y., G.R.]
Catharine [? Skiff], w. Vinal, Oct. 5, 1815, in 55th y. G.R.
Hannah, w. Elijah, June 23, 1790. [in 43d y., G.R.]
Joanna [? Skiff], w. Vinal, Mar. 7, 1827, a. 34. G.R.
Matthew, ch. Elijah and Hannah, Sept. 10, 1786.
Mayhew, ch. Elijah and Hannah, May 4, 1775.
Shobal, Apr. 5, 1733, in 81st y.
Shobal [h. Abigail], Apr. 4, 1754 [? 1734], in 80th y. G.R.
Vinal (see Vinal Skiff).

SPOFFORD, Ann Matilda, b. Brentwood, N.H., ch. Luke A. [and] Grata, consumption, July 1, 1843, a. 15 y. 9 m. 8 d.
Richard C., Rev., b. Bradford, s. Rev. Luke A. [and] Grata, consumption, May 25, 1843, a. 25 y. 5 m. 3 d. [Rev. Richard Cecil, G.R.]

STEWART, Jedidah, d. William, Apr. 5, 1848.
Mary, ch. Moses Lumbert and Sarah, old age, Oct. 25, 1849, a. 81.
Nathan, s. William and Ruhamah, Jan. 2, 1770, a. 8 y. 6 m. G.R.
Ruhamah, Mar. 10, 1823. G.R.
William, Dec. 24, 1824. G.R.
———, s. George W. and Jerusha, concumption, Aug. 16 [1843], a. 3 m. 27 d.

TILLTON (see Tilton), Beriah, July 10, 1779. [Tilton [h. Mary], in 76th y., G.R.]
Cyrano (see Sirano).
David, ch. Uriah and Jedidah, Sept. 14, 1796.
Elisha, ch. Uriah and Jedidah, Sept. 15, 1776. [Tilton, Sept. 14, in 37th y., G.R.]
Hannah, d. William and Bershabe, Apr. 11, 1778.
Jedidah, w. Uriah, Mar. 31, 1788. [Tilton, w. Capt. Uriah, in 68th y., G.R.]
Jonathan, ch. Uriah and Jedidah, Feb. 22, 1768.
Mary, w. Beriah, Sept. 16, 1778. [Tilton, in 65th y., G.R.]
Mary B. [w. Josiah], Jan. 1, 1827. [Tilton, July 1, a. 35, G.R.]
Mercy, ch. Uriah and Jedidah, May 27, 1768.
Sirano [ch. John (Tilton) and Sarah], Feb. 23, 1791.
Uriah Jr., ch. Uriah and Jedidah, Aug. 23, 1778.

CHILMARK DEATHS. 95

TILLTON, Uriah Sr. [h. Jedidah], Jan. 1, 1787. [Capt. Uriah Tilton, Jan. 1, 1788, in 74th y., G.R.]
William, father of Beriah, June —, 1750.
Zepheniah, ch. Uriah and Jedidah, Feb. 14, 1752.

TILTON (see Tillton), Abigail, w. Dea. Reuben, July 10, 1801, in 59th y. G.R.
Albert, s. Oliver and Eunice, Jan. 21, 1814, a. 22 y. 1 m. 16 d. G.R.
Anna, d. W[illia]m and Bathsheba, consumption, Oct. 1, 1849, a. 71.
Asa [h. Sarah], Dec. 25, 1834, a. 65. G.R.
Barsheba, wid. William, June 15, 1826, a. 82. G.R.
Beriah, decay of nature, Apr. 25, 1843, a. 79 y. 10 m. 18 d. [[h. Lydia] Apr. 24, a. 80, G.R.]
Daniel [h. Lavinia], Mar. 7, 1818, a. 46 y. 1 m. 1 d. G.R.
Daniel, May 3, 1839, a. 66. G.R.
Eliakim, June 15, 1796, in W.I. G.R.
Elisha, Aug. 20, 1781, in N.Y. G.R.
Elizabeth, w. Ezra, Aug. 10, 1776.
Eunice A., d. John and Mary, Aug. 20, 1837, a. 7. G.R.
Fanny, ch. William and Margaret, Nov. — [1802].
Francis, lost at sea, Sept. 15, 1785. G.R.
Francis, Capt., Sept. 17, 1827, in 42d y. G.R.
Francis B., June 8, 1839, a. 57. G.R.
Freeman, s. Oliver and Eunice, Dec. 22, 1806, a. 1 y. 2 m. 8 d. G.R.
Hannah, w. Samuel, Jan. 10, 1776, in 36th y. G.R.
Hannah [w. Josiah], ———. [This entry in pencil.]
Hugh Cathcart, s. Allen and Mary, Jan. 27, 1840, a. 4 y. 3 m. G.R.
Jedidah, w. David, Feb. 10, 1826, in 44th y. G.R.
Jemimah, w. Thomas, Sept. 15, 1761, in 41st y. G.R.
Jonathan, May 29, 1837. G.R.
Joseph [h. Ruth], Sept. 3, 1796, a. 85. G.R.
Julia, ch. Cornelius and Almira, Aug. 5, 1827, a. 6 hrs. G.R.
Levi, ch. Cornelius and Almira, Dec. 11, 1826, a. 14 m. 15 d. G.R.
Lydia, w. Beriah, Nov. —, 1840, a. 82. G.R.
Margaret [dup. (Stewart)] [dup. w. William], dysentary, Nov. 1, 1849, a. 82. [a. 83 y. 3 m. 21 d., G.R.]
Martha, w. David, Jan. 2, 1803, in 22d y. G.R.
Matthew [h. Sarah], July 25, 1830, a. 95 y. 2 m. 12 d. G.R.

TILTON, Oliver, m., s. Joseph and Zilpah, consumption, ———
[rec. May —, 1846], a. 30 y. 10 m. 14 d.
Olivia, lumbo abscess, Dec. 24, 1842, a. 22 y. 4 m. 6 d. [Olivia B., d. Cornelius and Almira, G.R.]
Rebecca, w. Capt. Samuel, June 18, 1816, a. 82 y. 9 m. 13 d. G.R.
Rebecca, w. Stephen, Oct. 23, 1829, a. 84. G.R.
Ruth, w. Joseph, Oct. —, 1740, in 27th y. G.R.
Salathiel, ———, 1807, at sea.
Samuel, s. Stephen and Rebecca, Apr. 8, 1770, a. 5 y. 19 d. G.R.
Samuel [h. Hannah], Apr. 3, 1778, in 56th y. G.R.
Sarah, w. Matthew, July 3, 1805, in 52d y. G.R.
Sarah, w. Asa, Mar. 3, 1826, in 51st y. G.R.
Sophia, ch. William and Margaret, Feb. 26, 1848.
Stephen [h. Rebecca], May 9, 1813, in 66th y. G.R.
Susan, dropsy of heart, Mar. 8 [? 1849], a. 51. [w. Benjamin S., Mar. 7, 1849, G.R.]
Thomas [h. Jemimah], Apr. 4, 1801, in 99th y. G.R.
William [h. Barsheba], June 27, 1818, a. 72. G.R.
Zeno, s. Daniel and Lavinia, Nov. 1, 1817, a. 18 y. 10 d., "on return voyage from the South sea." G.R.
Zilpha, w. Joseph, Feb. 18, 1809, a. 88. G.R.
———, s. William and Margaret, Apr. 8 [1793].
———, ch. Oliver, Dec. 22, 1806.
———, inf. John and Mary, Oct. 28, 1821. G.R.

VINCENT, Daniel, ch. Herman and Elizabeth, Nov. 11, 1840, a. 7 hrs. G.R.
Daniel, s. Herman and Louissa, July 10 [1845], a. 10 d. [ch. Herman and Elizabeth, July 10, 1844, G.R.]
George, ch. Herman and Elizabeth, June 10, 1835, a. 13 m. 26 d. G.R.
Louisa, ch. Herman and Elizabeth, Apr. 5, 1839, a. 7 d. G.R.
———, d. Herman and Louisa, still born, Apr. 7, 1846.

WEST, Lovey, July 9, 1790. G.R.
Sarah, w. Capt. Thomas, Jan. 31, 1816. G.R.
Thomas, Capt., lost at sea, Nov. —, 1816. G.R.
———, inf. s. Capt. Leonard and Rebecca, July 17, 1838. G.R.

WIMPENNY, Bathsheba, b. Tisbury, wid. William, d. Zaccheus Luce [and] Sarah, old age, Dec. 31, 1843, a. 88 y. 4 m. 18 d.

ADDITIONAL CHILMARK BIRTHS, MARRIAGES, AND DEATHS.

INTRODUCTION TO ADDITIONS

The following are additions to the *Vital Records of Chilmark, Massachusetts, to the Year 1850*, as printed in 1904 by the New England Historic Genealogical Society, Boston, Massachusetts.

The basic data is from a handwritten copy of the Chilmark Congregational Church Records 1787-1820, date and author unknown, in possession of the Dukes County Historical Society, Edgartown, Massachusetts. Some additional data is provided from penciled notes of William J. Rotch as well as a manuscript copy of Chilmark records by Alexander Graham Bell in his research on the deaf. A few other items were found in a copy of Chilmark Methodist Church records and depositions in the town records (see note below). All such additional material is coded to show the source. Entries which also appear in the 1904 publication are so noted.

ABBREVIATIONS AND CODES

ch - child of.
CTR - Chilmark Town Records, not found elsewhere (see NOTE below).
CVR - *Vital Records of Chilmark to 1850...*
d - daughter of, died.
(HMP) - in Harriet Marshall Pease Collection at Dukes County Historical Society, but not found elsewhere.
m - married
(M) - found in copy of Chilmark Methodist Church records and associated copy of "statistics" at Dukes County Historical Society, but not found elsewhere.

s - son of.

% - also appear in the published vital records (CVR).

@ - towns not included in CVR.

( ) - data from the published vital records which differs from these records.

* - also from penciled notes made by William J. Rotch in a copy of *Vital Records of Chilmark...* owned by the Dukes County Historical Society. Mr. Rotch wrote in the book that he found the information in old wills, deeds, diaries, and other historical documents.

[ ] - in the Rotch records but not the church records.

- from a manuscript *Complete Copy Births in Chilmark Records* by Alexander Graham Bell (also in the possession of the Dukes County Historical Society).

NOTE: The town of Chilmark has no vital records before 1845. There are occasional entries in the old town meeting reports which are included in CVR. The Chilmark Town Records herein are from individual depositions filed with the town clerk after 1850.

The towns of Chilmark, Edgartown, Gay Head and Tisbury are on the island of Martha's Vineyard in Dukes County, Massachusetts. Boston, New Bedford, Falmouth, Sandwich, Salem, Plympton and Plymouth are also in Massachusetts. Addison, Farmington, Hallowell, New Sharon and Unity are in Maine.

Catherine Merwin Mayhew
February 1991

BIRTH ADDITIONS

ADAMS, Elvira D, March 10, 1844 m James H Vincent % * {not in church records}
G Washington, s William and Thankful, July 8, 1808 (s William)%
___, ch William, 1796
___, ch Moses and Martha, 1799
___, ch James, 1799
___, ch William, Jan 3, 1800
___, d William, April 28?, 1802
___, s William and Thankful, June 22, 1805
___, d Moses and Martha Adams, Nov 8, 1808 (d Moses) %
___, s William and Thankful, July 17, 1810
___, s Moses and Martha, Sept 7, 1811
___, d William and Thankful, July 11, 1812
___, d Moses and Martha, Oct 24, 1814
___, s William and Thankful, Jan 14, 1815
___, d William, Oct 27, 1818

ALLEN, Adolphus, s James and Cynthia, Feb 23, 1806 (James Jr) %
Bartlett, s Matthew and Temperance, Sept 16, 1799 %
Bartlett, s William and Love, Aug 25, 1781 % *
Bulah D, ch Ephraim and Rebecca, Aug 29, 1811 %
Clorissa, d Tristram and Clarissa, Feb 26, 1814 %
Deborah, ch Tristram and Clarissa, Jan 24, 1807 %
[Dinah, d William and Love, Feb 13, 1785, m Rev Thos Merrill] *
[Eliza], d Ezra and Beulah, Sept 30, 1800 *
Ephraim, ch Ephraim and Rebecca, March 7, 1820 (March 2) %
Frederick, ch Tristram and Clarissa, Aug 26, 1811 (Aug 25) %

ALLEN, Hannah M, d Ephraim and Rebecca, Sept 10, 1809 %
Horace, s Zebulon and Prudence, Sept 7, 1804 (ch Sibulon) %
Jonah, s James and Abigail, Feb 13, 1763 # {not in church recs}
Jonathan, s Tristram and Clarissa, Oct 7, 1796 %
Joshua, s Zebulon and Prudence, Mar 10, 1800 (ch Sibulon) %
Julia, d Zebulon and Prudence, Feb 28, 1791 (ch Sibulon, Mar 1)%
Louisa, d Zebulon and Prudence, Nov 25, 1807 (ch Sibulon) %
Love, d William and Love, June 12, 1787 % [m John Robinson] *
Margaret C, d Ephraim Jr and Rebecca, July 16, 1813 (July 14)%
Mary Ann, d Tristram and Clarissa Jan 12, 1802 (Jan 13) %
Myra, d Zebulon and Prudence, Sept 25, 1794 (ch Sibulon) %
Patience, d Matthew and Patience, Oct 20, 1797 %
Rebecca, ch Ephraim and Rebecca, Jan 19, 1818 %
Sally Mayhew, d Zebulon and Prudence, July 10, 1797 (ch Sibulon) %
Samuel, ch Ephraim and Rebecca, Nov 17, 1815 (Nov 18) %
Sophronia, d Henry and Sophia, Oct 4, 1806 (d Henry, Oct 6) %
Thomas L, s Tristram and Clarissa, Feb 8, 1799 % {church record reads: "son 1799"}
Tristram, ch Tristram and Clarissa, Sept 5, 1804 %
Truman, s William and Love, June 19, 1783 % [d 1818] *
William, s William and Love, April 16, 1780 % *
Zach, s William and Sarah Mayhew, Feb 1746 # (Zachs or Zacheus, s William and Sarah, Feb 4, 1744-45) %
____, child stillborn Zebulon and Prudence
____, d John Allen Esq and Mary, Jan 8, 1790
____, d William and Love, May 16, 1790
____, s Salathiel and Lucy, Nov 13, 1790
____, s William and Love, Apr 26, 1792
____, d Salathiel and Lucy, May 12, 1792
____, ch Sylvanus and Catherine, Jan 17, 1794
____, ch Sylvanus and Catherine, Jan 4, 1795

ALLEN, ___, d Sylvanus and Catherine, Dec 22, 1795
___, s Sylvanus and Catherine, May 11, 1797
___, s Sylvanus and Catherine, Aug 1798
___, d Sylvanus and Patience (sic), Oct 12, 1799
___, s Henry and Sophia, 1802
___, d Matthew Allen March 12, 1802
___, d Sylvanus and Catherine, Nov 10, 1802
___, s Henry and Sophia, March 15, 1804
___, s James and Cynthia, Aug 3, 1804
___, d Sylvanus and Catherine, May 13, 1805
___, d James and Cynthia, Feb 23, 1806
___, s James and Cynthia, Jan 27, 1809
___, s Henry and Sophia, Sept 22, 1810
___, s James and Cynthia, Sept 9, 1811
___, d Henry and Sophia, May 5, 1814
___, d Henry and Sophia, Nov 1816

BASSETT/BASSITT, Anna, ch William and Olivia, July 8, 1803 %
Asahel, ch Ebenezer and Abigail, Nov 26, 1780 % [m Prudence Weston] *
Benjamin, [s John and Jean], Aug 1, 1752 % * (m Abigail Nickerson) %
[Ebenezer, s Cornelius, 1751, m Abigail Adams, removed to Easton, NY, 1799, children born Chilmark] *
Elizabeth, d John and Jean, May 16, 1736 % [m Ezra Tilton] *
Ephraim, s Samuel and Anna, May 7, 1780 # (Ephream Guld) %
Jonathan, ch Benjamin and Abigail, March 22, 1792 (March 20)%
Joseph, ch Joseph and Mary, Sept 15, 1788 %
Katharine, d Nathaniel Esq and Catherine, March 25, 1795 (Mar 26) %
Lydia Norton, ch Samuel and Anna, April 27, 1789 (April 28) %
Martha, ch Norton and Clarissa, Aug 28, 1792 (and Carrissa, Aug 29, 1792, in NY) %

BASSETT/BASSITT, Mary, ch William and Olivia, Aug 16, 1801 %

Mayhew, ch Joseph and Mary, Sept 22, 1792 (Sept 21) %

Nathan, ch William and Olivia, Aug 5, 1795 (Aug 4) %

Nathaniel, s Nathaniel and Catherine, June 3, 1789 (June 2) %

Perez, ch William and Olivia, June 1, 1797 %

[Peter Norton, Dec 1782, m Esther Broughton] *

Ruth, ch Benjamin and Abigail, Sept 3, 1789 (Sept 4) %

[Sarah, d Samuel and Martha, March 19, 1720, m Major Peter Norton 1740] *

[Sarah Adams, May 7, 1787, m Reuben Coffin formerly of Nantucket] *

Silas, ch Joseph and Mary, June 11, 1790 %

___, ch William and Olivia, June 1, 1797

___, s Nathan and Martha, April 9, 1788

___, s Nathan and Martha Aug 12, 1790

___, ch Ebenezer, Nov 14, 1790

___, d Nathaniel and Catherine, Jan 11, 1791

___, ch Ebenezer, Jan or Feb 1792

___, ch Ebenezer, 1794

___, ch Ebenezer, 1796

___, ch Ebenezer, 30 June 1797

___, d Benjamin and Prudence, Nov 29, 1811

___, s Benjamin and Prudence, Dec 12, 1813

BOARDMAN, twin d Walter and Jane, Aug 26, 1791
twin s Walter and Jane, Aug 26, 1791

BUTLER, Frederick Norton, s Nicholas and Lucy, June 10, 1791 %

[Nathaniel, s Israel, bapt June 8, 1726] *

___, d Athearn and Desire, July 21, 1789

___, d Athearn and Desire, May 6, 1791

___, ch Nicholas and Lucy, 1793

___, ch Nicholas and Lucy, 1799

[**CHASE**, Thomas, Dec 22, 1721] *

CHESBROUGH, Augustus N, s Henry W and Sophronia, Sept 1844 # {not in church records}

CLARK, [Mary, d of "Mrs Clark," bapt Oct 10, 1721] *
____, d of William, Nov 2, 1812

COFFIN, Love, born Edgartown, May 3, 1756 # {not in church rec}
____, ch Matthew and Betsy, March 1800

COTTLE, Abram Williams, s William and Anne, Sept 7, 1808, (s Wm) %
[Cynthia C, d Silas and Jerusha, May 17, 1789] *
[Elizabeth, d John, bapt June 8, 1726] *
[Francis, s Silas and Jerusha, Dec 3, 1787] *
Jerusha, d Mayhew and Sally, Oct 22, 1805 (m George W Stuart) % {parents not listed in CVR}
[Mayhew, s Silas and Jerusha, Dec 8, 1779, d Feb 10, 1870] *
[Sally, d Silas and Jerusha, Oct 8, 1782, d Apr 26, 1872] *
Sally Dunham, d Mayhew and Sally, June 27, 1807 (d Mayhew)%
Truman, June 27, 1794
____, ch John and Rebecca, Jan 1788
____, d John and Rebecca, Oct 15, 1788
____, d Silas and Jerusha, May 17, 1789
____, d John and Rebecca, Sept 30, 1791
____, s Jeremiah and Rebecca, June 27, 1794
____, ch Mayhew and Sally, May 27, 1809
____, s William, Oct 14, 1810
____, d William and Anne, March 24, 1813
____, s Mayhew and Sally, March 26, 1813

COTTLE, ___, d Mayhew and Sally, Aug 22, 1813 (sic)
___, d Mayhew and Sally, Nov 25, 1815
___, d Mayhew and Sally, Dec 20, 1818

COX, ___, ch Thomas and Sarah, Oct 1789
___, d Thomas and Sarah, Nov 13, 1791
___, s Thomas, Jan 23, 1795
___, ch Thomas, Jan 29, 1800

CROWELL, ___, s Samuel, Jan 26, 1814

DOUGLASS, ___, s Experience, Feb 15, 1803

FERGUSON, ___, ch William, Nov 1794
___, ch William, Oct 1796
___, ch William, May 6, 1799
___, d William, March 29, 1802
___, ch William, April 3, 1804

FLANDERS, Almira, ch John and Hannah, Oct 17, 1795 (Oct 16) %
Alvin, ch John and Hannah, July 13, 1794 %
Daniel, ch John and Hannah, Nov 9, 1801 (Nov 6) %
Hannah, d John and Hannah Flanders, Apr 15, 1799 (m Josiah Tilton) %
John, s John and Hannah, 1797 (May 1 or 18) %
Rebecca, ch John and Hannah, June 29, 1806 (w Leonard West)%
Robert N, s Samuel and Keziah Lumbert, Oct 10, 1850 CTR
___, s John and Hannah, March 29, 1804
___, s John and Hannah, June 4, 1809
___, s John and Hannah, Jan 12, 1812

[**FOSTER**, Hannah, ch Joseph, bapt Oct 16, 1740] *

GOFF, Ann, d William and Lydia, Feb 20, 1846 # % {not in church recs}

GOULD, Cecila, d Horace and Polly, Feb 3, 1806 (d Horace) %

GREEN, ___, d Timothy and Hannah?, March 1793

HANCOCK, Margaret, d James, Apr 19 1800 (parent not in CVR, m George D) %
Sophronia A, d Cyrus H and Thankful Manter, Aug 7, 1846, CTR
___, ch James, 1794
___, ch James, 1796
___, d James, July 8, 1798
___, s James, Aug 19, 1800
___, s James, Dec 6, 1802
___, s Betsy, April 22, 1805
___, d Samuel, Oct 21, 1807 %
___, d Samuel, Dec 12, 1809
___, s Samuel and Fanny, June 15, 1813
___, d John, Dec 12, 1814
___, d John, July 21, 1818
___, ch Cyrus and Thankful, Nov 1848 # {not in church records}

HARTLAND, d Elijah and Sophronia, Dec 1848 # {not in church records}

HATCH, ___, d Reuben and Lucy, Aug 2, 1790
___, ch Reuben, 1792
___, s Reuben and Lucy, March 28, 1792
___, ch Cyrus and Betsy, May 28, 1792
___, s Cyrus and Betsy, Apr 14, 1794

HILLMAN, Benjamin, ch Ezra and Zerniah, Apr 3, 1793 (Apr 2)%

HILLMAN, Betsy Chase, ch Moses and Lydia, Apr 5, 1806 %
Charlotte, ch Moses and Lydia, Jan 7, 1803 %
Charlotte J, d Owen and Charlotte, May 17, 1846, (m John
    Wesley Mayhew) % *
Jamey, s Robert and Rebecca, Aug 16, 1781/1783 # (James, Aug
    15) %
Josiah, s Robert and Rebecca, June 19, 1773 #
Jonathan (2nd), s Samuel and Sheba/Phebe ? (sic), Sept 6, 1757
    # %
Lydia, ch Moses and Lydia, Dec 8, 1804 (Dec 3) %
Matty, ch Ezra and Zerviah, Apr 14, 1789 (and Zerniah, Apr
    16)%
Pardon, s Elizabeth Hillman, 1787 # (Oct 15, 1787) %
Susanna, d Owen and Polly, June 7, 1797, (m Benj S Tilton,
    parents not in CVR) %
Thurston ? (sic), ch Samuel and Phebe ? (sic), Jan 16, 1752 #
Tristram, ch Samuel and Pheba, July 16, 1752) % {not in church
    records}
Tristram, ch Moses and Lydia, Aug 14, 1795 %
____, ch Edward and Lydia, 1788
____, d Thomas and Ruth, Sept 6, 1788
____, d Benjamin and Mary, Nov 10, 1790
____, s Thomas and Ruth, March 20, 1791
____, s Edward and Lydia, Apr 27, 1791
____, s Thomas and Ruth, Oct 18, 1792
____, d Thomas and Ruth, June 26, 1795
____, s Moses and Lydia, Apr 2, 1797
____, ch Uriel and Betsey, July 14, 1798
____, ch Moses and Lydia, Sept 5, 1798
____, s Owen and Polly, Dec 5, 1798
____, ch Uriel, 1800
____, d Moses and Lydia, Jan 5, 1801
____, d Prince and Nancy, May 27, 1802
____, d Rebecca, Dec 14, 1802
____, s Moses and Lydia, Sept 1, 1808 (s Mosis, Sept 7?) %

HILLMAN, ___, d Stephen and Bathsheba, July 31, 1809
___, ch Moses and Lydia, 1810
___, d Owen and Polly, Apr 21, 1811
___, d Owen and Polly, Feb 23, 1813
___, s Moses and Lydia, March 15, 1814
___, d Owen and Polly, Apr 10, 1815
___, d Owen and Polly, Oct 4, 1818

HUNT, [Abiah, d William, bapt July 5, 1719, first child] *
[Jane, d William, bapt Aug 18, 1723] *
[Hannah, d William, bapt July 10, 1726] *
[Sarah, d William, bapt July 10, 1726] *

JOHNSON, ___, ch Susanna, Aug 7, 1800
___, s Asa and Prudence, March 11, 1817
___, d Asa and Prudence, March 28, 1819

JONES, (Polly, ch Daniel and Mary, July 4, 1788) % {church records read "son, July 5, 1788"}
Zerviah (M), d Ebenezer and Sukey, Jan 16, 1794 {Jan 19 (M)}

LAMBERT/LUMBERT, Frederick H, s Thomas H and Lydia West, Oct 19, 1845 (Sept 1845) CTR
Thomas H, s Thomas and Parnell, April 8, 1795 (hus Deborah A)%
___, d Thomas and Parnell, Sept 7, 1792
___, d Thomas and Parnell, May 17, 1797
___, ch Abishai, 1798
___, ch Francis, 1799
___, ch Abishai, June 1801
___, d Thomas and Parnell, Jan 1, 1802
___, s Thomas and Parnell, Oct 14, 1804
___, d Thomas and Parnell, Jan 17, 1808
___, d Abishai, Aug 4, 1818

LEWIS, ____, d John, Oct 9, 1818

LOOK, Alfred Herbert, s Alfred and Jane Cottle, Feb 21, 1849 CTR
Moses, s Prince and Sarah, Jan 7, 1791 (parents not in CVR) %
Reuben, s Prince and Sarah, Jan 29, 1789 (Jan 15, parents not in CVR) %
Sarah, d Job, July 26, 1794 (parents not in CVR) %
____, s Lot and Susanna, April 3, 1791
____, d Prince and Sarah, July 14, 1793
____, ch Prince and Sarah, Oct 30, 1795
____, ch George and Persis, 1805
____, d George and Persis, Feb 19, 1807 (d George) %
____, d George and Persis, Sept 14, 1808 (d George) %
____, d George and Persis, Apr 30, 1810
____, d Aaron, May 4, 1816

LUCE, ____, d Benjamin and Damaris, May 9, 1788
____, s Shubael and Hannah, June 14, 1789
____, s Alsberry and Sarah, Aug 1791
____, ch Zephaniah, 1794
____, s Daniel and Abigail, Jan 18, 1806 (s Daniel) %
____, s Daniel and Abigail, May 21, 1807 (s Daniel) %
____, s Daniel and Abigail, Dec 5, 1808 (s Daniel) %
____, s Daniel and Abigail, Aug 28, 1810
____, d Daniel and Abigail, Jan 21, 1812
____, d Ebenezer, Apr 27, 1817
____, d Ebenezer, Dec 16, 1818
____, ch David, 1820

MANTER, ____, d Samuel, Nov 20, 1802
____, d Jeremiah and Elizabeth, Oct 11, 1819
____, s Granville and Catherine Mayhew, Apr 1, 1844 (Apr 1844) CTR

MANTER, ___, d Granville and Catherine Mayhew, Jan 15, 1848 (son) CTR

MAYHEW, Alfred, s Benjamin and Lydia, Jan 30, 1805 (parents not in CVR) %
Andrew Boardman, s widow Abigail, Sept 9, 1791 (ch Nathan and Abigail) %
[Bathsheba, d Timothy, bapt Aug 10, 1740] *
Caroline, d Dr Allen and Eunice, Sept 1800 % #
Catherine Cottle, d Abner and Eunice, April 27, 1810 [m Granville Manter] *
Deidamia Tilton, d Abner and Eunice, July 15, 1814 [July 14, 1814, m Joseph Mayhew Jr] *
Ebon ? (sic), s Simon and Milda, Feb 2, 1749 # {not in church records}
[Eliza Lowell, d Abner and Eunice, Mar 22, 1824, m Josiah Mayhew] *
Elizabeth, d Thomas Wade and Parnell, Jan 20, 1793 (Jan 8) %
Ephaniah, s Zephaniah and Hannah, 1745 # {not in church records}
Frederick*, s David and Patty, Sept 11, 1808 (___, s David) %
Gilbert, s Parnell, Aug 25, 1800 (ch Jonathan and Parnal) %
Hannah, ch Ephraim and Jedidah, July 1794 (July 7, 1794) %
Hannah, d Pain and Mary, March 31, 1713-14 % ; d June 1715
[Hannah, d Timothy, bapt Aug 10, 1740] *
Hannah G, d Elijah and Asenath, Feb 1848 # {not in church records}
Hebron, ch Hebron and Deborah, July 5, 1793 %
Hillyard, twin s Ephraim and Jedidah, Mar 18, 1791 (March 19)%
Homes, ch Willmott and Nancey, Aug 24, 1787 %
James, ch Nathan and Abigail, Oct 15, 1789 (Oct 16) %
James Hillman, s Abner and Eunice, Aug 9, 1820 [m Mary S Cottle]*
Jane, d Simon and Abiah, Aug 28 1768 #; d same day #

MAYHEW, [Jane Vincent, d Josiah and Eliza L, no date] *
Jeremiah, twin s Ephraim and Jedidah, Mar 18, 1791 (March 19) %
Jonathan, ch Jonathan and Parnell, April 1797 (April 7, 1797) %
Love /Lucy, d Pain and Dinah, Apr 7, 1745 (M)
Lucinda, d Ephraim and Lucinda Poole, June 13, 1817 (m Ephraim) %
[Lucy, d Nathan and Abigail, Sept 18, 1782] *
Mary J, d Tristram and Jane Nickerson, Dec 23, 1850 CTR
[Matilda Vincent, d Abner and Eunice, Sept 30, 1816 m Charles F Dunham] *
Milda, d Simon and Milda, Aug 1755 # {not in church records}
Mira, ch Hebron and Deborah, April 8, 1798 (April 9) %
Nancy Smith, d Abner and Eunice, Feb 25, 1812 [Feb 27, m John Dunham] *
Nathan, ch Hebron and Deborah, Oct 8, 1795 (Oct 9) %
Philip S, ch Ephraim and Jedidah, July 13, 1797 %
Philip Smith, s Abner and Eunice, Dec 3, 1818 [Oct 3, m Caroline Rogers] *
Rebecca, ch Jonathan and Parnell, June 18, 1795 %
[Rachel, d Timothy, bapt Aug 10, 1740] *
[Reliance, d Timothy, bapt Aug 10, 1740] *
[Sarah, d Capt Zacheus, bapt March 1, 1719] *
Simon, s Simon and Milda, Nov 15, 1753 # %
Smith, ch Ephraim and Jedidah, Sept 22, 1788 (Sept 23) %
[Tamson B], d Abner and Eunice, July 18, 1808 (____, d Abner) % [July 19, m Roland Luce] *
{Thankful}, d David and Patty, Nov 6, 1806 (____, d David) %
Theodore Allen, s Dr Allen and Eunice, Jan 3, 1797 (Jan 4) %
Tristram, s David, Oct 18, 1810 (m Jane N) %
Unice, d Experience and Remember, Apr 4, 1716 % [m Moses Belcher] *
William B, s William B and Prudence, March 10, 1806 (s William B) %
____, ch Zaccheus and Pamela, b 1788

MAYHEW, ____, d Matthew and Rebecca, May 25, 1788
____, s Nathaniel and Mary, June 27, 1788
____, ch Timothy and Ruth, Aug 1788
____, ch Zaccheus and Pamela, 1788
____, d of Thomas Wade and Parnell, May 7, 1789
____, ch Benjamin, 1790
____, stillborn ch of Francis, 1790
____, s Zaccheus and Pamela, Oct 16, 1790
____, ch Benjamin, b 1790
____, d John and Hannah, Jan 27, 1791
____, s Matthew and Rebecca, Feb 17, 1791
____, s Francis and Susanna, Aug 1791
____, s Benjamin and Lydia, Nov 6, 1791
____, d Nathaniel and Mary, Apr 12, 1792
____, s John and Hannah, July 8, 1793
____, s Benjamin and Lydia, July 28, 1793
____, s Matthew Jr and Rebecca, (Sept) 1794
____, s Nathaniel and Mary, Oct 26, 1794
____, s Thomas Wade and Parnell, Dec 22, 1794
____, ch Benjamin Esq and Lydia, b 1795
____, d William and Phebe, Nov 8 ? (sic), 1795
____, ch Zephaniah, b 1796
____, ch John, June 1796
____, d Nathaniel and Polly, Nov 1796
____, ch Zephaniah, 1796
____, twin d Matthew and Rebecca, July 22, 1797
____, twin d Matthew and Rebecca, July 22, 1797
____, d John and Hannah, Nov 26, 1797
____, s William and Phebe, March 14, 1798
____, s Nathaniel and Polly, 1799
____, d Benjamin Esq and Lydia, July 1799
____, ch John, Jan 13, 1800
____, s Hebron and Deborah, Sept 11, 1800
____, ch William and Phebe, Oct 26, 1800
____, ch Zephaniah, Apr 26, 1801

MAYHEW, ____, d Nathaniel and Polly, June 30, 1801
____, d William and Phebe, June 30, 1801
____, d William B and Prudence, Aug 9, 1801
____, ch Benjamin, Esq, (April) 1802
____, s Seth and Betsy, Apr 24, 1802
____, ch Benjamin, Esq, (April) 1802
____, s Hebron and Deborah, June 4, 1803
____, s William B and Prudence, June 23, 1803
____, s William and Phebe, Oct 23, 1803
____, s Nathaniel and Polly, Dec 19, 1803
____, d William B and Prudence, Feb 20, 1804
____, d Seth and Betsy, Apr 23, 1804
____, d Joseph and Jedidah, Oct 1, 1804
____, s Zephaniah, Nov 14, 1804
____, s Benjamin Esq and Lydia, Jan 30, 1805
____, d Hebron and Deborah, Sept 21, 1805
____, s William B and Prudence, March 10, 1806
____, d Ephraim Jr and Sukey, Apr 27, 1806 (d Ephraim Jr) %
____, d William and Phebe, Aug 17, 1806 (d William) %
____, d Seth and Betsy, Sept 7, 1806 (d Seth) %
____, s Benjamin and Lydia, May 27, 1807 %
____, d Joseph and Jedidah, July 7, 1807 %
____, s Ephraim and Sukey, Sept 17, 1808 %
____, d William and Phebe, Jan 30, 1809
____, d Seth and Betsy, Feb 3, 1809
____, dau William B and Prudence, Feb 20, 1809
____, s Benjamin and Lydia, March 1809 (inf s, March 19, 1809)%
____, d Ephraim and Susanna, Apr 15, 1810
____, s Zephaniah, June 21, 1810
____, s David, Oct 18, 1810
____, s Seth and Betsy, May 11, 1811
____, ch William B and Prudence, Aug 10, 1811
____, s William and Phebe, Oct 4, 1811
____, s Thomas W and Lucy, Dec 10, 1811

MAYHEW, ___, s Joseph and Jedidah, Apr 13, 1812
___, d David and Polly, Dec 25, 1812
___, d Frederick and Ethelinda, Feb 26, 1813
___, s Zephaniah, Dec 4, 1813
___, s Thomas W and Lucy, Dec 31, 1813
___, s Malatiah, Jan 16, 1814
___, d William B and Prudence, Feb 2, 1814
___, s William and Phebe, July 24, 1814
___, s Hebron and Prudence, Sept 20, 1814
___, d Ephraim and Susan, May 16, 1815
___, d David and Patty, June 3, 1815
___, s Joseph, April 3, 1816
___, d Thomas Wade and Lucy, Sept 4, 1816
___, s Zephaniah, Oct 20, 1816
___, s William B and Prudence, Jan 8, 1817
___, d William and Phebe, Jan 29, 1817
___, d David and Patty, June 6, 1817
___, s Meltiah, March 31, 1818
___, s Joseph, Sept 2, 1818
___, s William B, Oct 19, 1818
___, s George, Nov 8, 1818
___, s Thomas W and Lucy, May 13, 1819
___, s William and Phebe, Sept 15, 1819
___, d David and Martha, Oct 14, 1819
___, d Davis, Sept 27, 1820
___, s Joseph, Dec 18 1820
___, d Josiah and Eliza, March 20, 1846 #

MCCOLLUM, Martha, d Archibald and Patty, Apr 19, 1808 (d Arehable)%
___, s Archibald and Patty, July 11, 1800
___, s Archibald, May 23, 1802
___, s Archibald and Patty, Aug 1, 1803
___, d Archibald, Apr 28, 1806
___, d Archibald, Sept 13, 1810

MCCOLLUM, ___, d Archibald and Patty, July 14, 1812
___, s Archibald and Patty, Apr 5, 1815
___, d Archibald and Patty, Feb 3, 1817

NICKERSON, Samuel, s Samuel and Jane, Sept 2, 1803 (m
    Clarissa Hillman) %
___, s Nathaniel and Lydia, Nov 23, 1788
___, s Samuel and Jane, Oct 5, 1790
___, ch Nathaniel and Lydia, May 11, 1791

NORTON, Elizabeth, d William and Polly, Nov 26, 1796 (Nov
    26) %
James William, ch William and Polly, Dec 17, 1794 (Dec 18) %
Mary B, d William and Polly Norton, Dec 29, 1792 (m Josiah
    Tilton) %
William, ch Samuel and Eunice, April 26, 1812 (Apr 28, m
    Martha G Bassett) %
___, s Shubael and Love, Nov 1791
___, d Shubael and Love, Aug 10, 1796
___, s Shubael and Love, March 11, 1798
___, s William and Polly, Sept 1798
___, ch Shubael and Love, 1799
___, s Shubael and Love, 1800
___, ch Shubael and Love, 1801
___, d Shubael and Love, Sept 25, 1803
___, s Thomas and Lavinia, Sept 15, 1807 (Thomas of Edgartown) %
___, twin s Samuel and Eunice, Aug 3, 1816 %
___, twin d Samuel and Eunice, Aug 3, 1816 (twin s) %

PACKARD, Rebecca [Hillman], July 30, 1785 % *
___, twin s William and Rebecca, June 15, 1815
___, twin s William and Rebecca, June 15, 1815

PEASE, ___, d Abishai Jr and Mary, March 1, 1789
___, d John and Hannah, June 19, 1789
___, d Fortunatus Jr, Apr 12, 1791
___, ch Fortunatus Jr, Oct 11, 1792
___, s Fortunatus and Rose, Feb 18, 1795
___, s Fortunatus and Rose, May 9, 1796
___, d Nathaniel and Elizabeth, Aug 7, 1796
___, ch Fortunatus and Rose, May 11, 1797
___, d Nathaniel and Elizabeth, Sept 14, 1797
___, ch Nathaniel and Elizabeth, Aug 25, 1799
___, ch Nathaniel, 1801
___, ch Fortunatus and Rose, March 27, 1801
___, s Fortunatus and Rose, Jan 15, 1803
___, ch Nathaniel and Elizabeth, June 8, 1803
___, ch Jeremiah, Feb 22, 1804
___, s Nathaniel and Elizabeth, June 27, 1804
___, d Fortunatus and Rose, Jan 10, 1806 (d Fortunatus Jr) %
___, ch Nathaniel and Elizabeth, Oct 12, 1807
___, d Jeremiah, Jan 18, 1809
___, ch Jeremiah, 1810
___, d Nathaniel and Elizabeth, Apr 4, 1810
___, twin s Nathaniel and Elizabeth, Feb 1813
___, twin d Nathaniel and Elizabeth, Feb 1813
___, d Nathaniel and Elizabeth, June 25, 1814
___, s Jeremiah and Nancy, March 13, 1815
___, ch Jeremiah, Oct 1818

PIANIT ?, Jonathan, s Elisha and Mary, May 11, 1728 (M)
Joseph, s Elisha and Mary, May 31, 1731 (M)
Margate, d Elisha and Mary, July 9, 1726 (M)
Mary, d Elisha and Mary, Feb 11, 1727 (M)

POOL/POOLE, Ellen M, d Ephraim and Martha Mayhew,
    March 8, 1849 CTR
Ephraim, Aug 9, 1773 CTR

POOL/POOLE, Ephraim, s Ephraim and Lucinda Tilton, Aug 3, 1813 %
(Jane S, d Ephraim and Lucinda Tilton, July 25, 1815) % {church records read "son b July 24, 1815}
Jane S, d Ephraim and Lucinda Tilton, Mar 17, 1819 %
Lucinda, d Ephraim and Lucinda Tilton, June 13, 1817 % {m Ephraim Mayhew}
Mary Mayhew, d Ephraim and Polly, July 18, 1806 (d Ephraim)%
Matthew, s Ephraim and Lucinda Tilton, Aug 18, 1810 (Aug 16)%
Parnel T, d Ephraim and Lucinda Tilton, Apr 21, 1812 (Apr 20)%
___, ch William and Bathsheba, Oct 1799
___, d Ephraim and Martha, March 1849 # {not in church records}

ROBINSON Martha, d John and Jane Robinson, Aug 8, 1808 (Robertson) %
___, d Jethro and Jane, Feb 16, 1813
___, s John and Jane, Dec 24, 1814
___, s John and Jane, Dec 11, 1816
___, s John and Jane, Sept 8, 1819

SKIFF/SKIFFE, Catharine, ch Vinal and Catharine, Aug 1794 (Aug 8) %
Joseph, s Ebenezer and Deborah, Oct 31, 1792 (Nov 1) %
Joseph, s Nathan and Marcy, Nov 18, 1707 # (Nov 18, 1709) % {not in church records}
Marcy, d Nathan and Marcy, July 5, 1701 # (Mercy) % {not in church records}
Robert, s William and Lydia, Aug 16, 1844 # {not in church records}
Rufus, s Ebenezer and Deborah, May 15, 1794 %
___, s Ebenezer and Deborah, Jan 26, 1797

SKIFF/SKIFFE, ___, ch Stephen and Bathsheba, 1811
___, s Stephen and Bathsheba, March 14, 1815
___, s Stephen, Dec 28, 1818

SMITH, (Elijah, ch Elijah and Hannah, June 29, 1771) % [s of
       Elijah and Bethia of Edgartown] * {not in church records}
Eloisa, d Rev Jonathan and Anna, Jan 13, 1791 % {see Elijah}
Elijah, s Rev Jonathan and Anna, Jan 1791 # {see Eloisa}
Erastus, s Rev Jonathan and Anna, Nov 1793 (Nov 1) %
___, d Mayhew and Sally, Sept 1, 1804
___, d Mayhew and Sally, Oct 1, 1806 (d Mayhew) %
___, s Mayhew and Sally, Apr 27, 1808
___, d Mayhew and Sally, Oct 4, 1809
___, d Mayhew and Sally, 1811
___, s Mayhew and Sally, March 14, 1816
___, d Shubael and Deidamia, Jan 28, 1817
___, s Mayhew and Sally, July 26, 1818
___, d Mayhew and Sally, Dec 2, 1819
___, s Samuel and Eunice, Aug 1849 # {not in church records}

STEWART, ___, d William and Bathsheba, Oct 29, 1789
___, s Jeremiah and Mary, Aug 30, 1791
___, s William and Bathsheba, Nov 20, 1791
___, ch William and Bathsheba, Feb 9, 1794
___, d Jeremiah and Polly, March 1, 1796
___, d William and Bathseba, March 9, 1800
___, s Polly, Oct 13, 1800
___, s William and Bathsheba, Jan 2, 1803
___, d William Jr and Bathsheba, May 12, 1806 (d William
    Jr)%
___, s William and Bathsheba, Feb 8, 1809
___, d William and Bathsheba, March 10, 1812
___, twin dead, William and Bathsheba, Oct 27, 1820
___, twin dead, William and Bathsheba, Oct 27, 1820

TAYLOR, [Nathaniel, s Barnabas, bapt Aug 7, 1726] *
____, s Anderson and Persis, Sept 7, 1791

THAXTER, ____, s John, Oct 21, 1820

TILTON /TILLTON, Albert, ch Oliver and Eunice, Dec 4, 1791 (Dec 5)%
Bathsheba, d Sirano and Remember, June 2, 1772 (M)
Benjamin S, s Beriah and Lydia, March 28, 1788 (March 23/28)%
Beriah, s William and Abiah, Oct 13, 1703 * % {not in church records}
[Calvin, s David and Jedidah, Oct 3, 1817] *
Charlotte, d Beriah and Lydia, June 8, 1804 (parents not in CVR, m Capt Owen Hillman Jr) %
Cornelius, ch Matthew and Sarah, March 23, 1789 (March 25) %
David, [s David and Jedidah] *, Sept 26, 1813 % {church records: ____, ch David and Jedidah, 1813}
[Deborah, d David and Jedidah, March 3, 1823] *
Elizabeth, d David and Matty, Jan 24, 1801 (d David and Martha) %
Fanny, ch William and Margaret, April 23, 1802 (Aug 22/23, m Norton Bassett Jr) %
Hebron, ch Matthew and Sarah, Aug 24, 1787 [to Zanesville OH 1818]*
[James R, s David and Jedidah, July 13, 1811] *
[Jane, d of William and Abiah, Aug 2, 1697] *
John, ch Oliver and Eunice, Aug 18, 1796 (Aug 19) %
[John, s Samuel, Oct 23, 1670 {NH records}] *
[Josiah, s Samuel, born about 1675 Chilmark] *
Julinia, ch Oliver and Eunice, Aug 8, 1800 %
Katharine ch Ezra and Mary, Apr 27 1802 (Aug 28) %
Lucinda, ch Matthew and Sarah, Feb 23, 1791 %
Margaret, ch William and Margaret, Apr 12, 1794 %
[Martha, d David and Jedidah, Dec 8, 1815] *

TILTON/TILLTON, Meribah, ch Oliver and Eunice, Apr 12, 1798 %
Pamelia, ch Oliver and Eunice, Jan 2, 1795 (Jan 3) %
Parnel, ch Matthew and Sarah, Feb 18, 1794 %
[Rachel, d Samuel, 1683 Chilmark] *
Ruhamah, ch William and Margaret, Sept 23, 1799 (Sept 22) %
Ruth, d Thomas and Jemima, Aug 27, 1743 # {not in church records}
Samuel, ch Matthew and Sarah, Aug 18, 1796 %
[Shadrach, s David and Jedidah, Mar 20, 1820] *
Sophia, ch William and Margaret, Feb 12, 1788 %
Theresa, ch William and Margaret, Apr 28, 1797 %
Warren M, s Beriah and Lydia, Nov 9, 1798 (parents not in CVR) %
William, s Beriah and Mary (Mayhew), June 13, 1739 # (no birthdate in CVR) % {not in church records}
William, ch William and Margaret, Oct 29, 1790 (Oct 28) %
[William, s Samuel, Nov 11, 1668 {NH records}] *
William, s William and Bathsheba, [June 13, 1739]* (no birthdate) %
___, s Ward and Elizabeth, Nov 29, 1788
___, s Joseph Jr and Deidemia, June 4, 1789
___, d Beriah and Lydia, Sept 24, 1790
___, d Ward and Elizabeth, Oct 25, 1790
___, d Pain and Susanna, Jan 16, 1791
___, d Beriah and Lydia, March 18, 1792
___, s William and Peggy, Apr 4, 1793 (and Margaret, Apr 5) %
___, ch Joseph Jr, 1793
___, d Isaac and Jemima, Jan 6, 1794
___, s Beriah and Lydia, Sept 22, 1794
___, ch Joseph Jr, Sept 1795
___, s Isaac and Jemima, 1796
___, ch Beriah and Lydia, Aug 9, 1796
___, ch Ward and Elizabeth, Sept 12, 1796
___, ch Joseph Jr, 1797

TILTON/TILLTON, ___, s Daniel and Lavinia, May 10, 1797
___, s Joseph Jr, 1799
___, ch Daniel and Lavinia, 1799
___, s Ward and Elizabeth, May 1800
___, d Daniel and Lavinia, July 25, 1802
___, s William Jr and Peggy, Aug 25, 1807
___, s Thomas and Fear, Oct 27, 1807 (s Thomas) %
___, d Daniel and Lavinia, 1809
___, d Ward Jr, March 2, 1814
___, s Ward and Anne, June 1, 1815
___, s William Jr, June 17, 1818
___, ch Beriah, 1820

VINCENT, ___, s Nathaniel, Nov 22, 1809

WEST, Emma L, March 25, 1850, d Moses and Rebecca CTR
George, s George and Prudence, Jan 27, 1817 (m Deidemia) %
Leonard, s George and Prudence, Nov 20, 1797 (Nov 21, m Rebecca Flanders) %
Lovey d Thomas and Sarah, June 7 1789 (July 7, parents not in CVR)%
Lydia, ch George and Prudence, Nov 27, 1806 %
Mary, ch George and Prudence, May 15, 1800 (May 13) %
Sophrona, ch George and Prudence, Apr 13, 1804 %
___, ch Thomas, Mar 18, 1796
___, d George, Apr 1809
___, d George and Prudence, Dec 7, 1811
___, d George and Prudence, Sept 23, 1812
___, d Love, Apr 5, 1818
___, d George and Prudence, Nov 13, 1819
___, ch Moses and Rebecca, Aug 3, 1846 # {not in church records}

MARRIAGE ADDITIONS

_____, Dick and Meriah, negroes belonging to Samuel Norton, Esq, Feb 27, 1736 *

ADAMS, [Abigail and Ebenezer Bassett, May 21, 1780] % *
[Ebenezer s Col Cornelius Bassett; settled in NY state] *
Betsy and Uriel Hillman, Dec 21, 1797 %
[Eliashib and Reliance Mayhew, Feb 18, 1729] *
Louisa and Thomas Norton of Edgartown, Oct 26, 1806 (Lovisa) % @
Susanna and Samuel Athearn, April 21, 1791 %

ALLEN, [Abigail and John Sturgis, Sept 5, 1728] *
[Benjamin and Abia Mayhew, Jan 8, 1730] *
Betsey of Chilmark and Matthew Coffin of Edgartown, Feb 21, 1799 % @
Catharine and Rev Andrew Boardman, Oct 8, 1747 (M)
Desire Jr and Athearn Butler, Oct 2, 1788 %
[Elizabeth and Zachariah Mayhew, Nov 21, 1738] *
Eunice and Dr Allen Mayhew, Dec 18, 1795 % *
[Eliza and Gerard Hallock, June 2, 1825] *
[Hannah and Elnathan Wing, Oct 7, 1726] *
Hannah of Chilmark and William Lawrence of Falmouth, Nov 5, 1801 % @
Henry of Chilmark and Sophia Spaulding of Tisbury, Feb 19, 1801 % @
Hepzibah and Capt Richard Luce, Jan 9, 1817
James 2nd and Cynthia Cottle, Nov 15, 1803 (int Aug 20, James 3rd)
[Jane and Handly Chipman, Apr 24, 1740] *

ALLEN, Jane and John Robinson, July 25, 1807 %
[Jethro and Dinah Mayhew, March 25, 1736] *
[Joshua and Agnes Homes, Dec 14, 1725] *
[Kathren and Capt David Moore, Aug 3, 1738] *
[Lucy and Thomas W Mayhew, Dec 23, 1810] *
[Martha and Barnabas Taylor, Nov 4, 1725] *
Martha Jr and Capt William Worth Sept 25 1788 (Martha, Apr 5 1788)
Mary, Mrs and Shubael Cottle, Esq, June 9, 1803 (int May 26)
Matthew of Chilmark and Temperance Allen of Tisbury, Nov 29, 1798 % @
Nancy and Rev Nymphas Hatch, Apr 22, 1802 *
Nancy and Nathaniel Mayhew, Dec 12, 1815 *
Persis and George Look of Tisbury, Nov 27, 1800 % @
Prudence, and William B Mayhew, Nov 6, 1800 % {church records Mrs Allen}
[Rebecca and Wilmot Wass, March 22, 1733] *
Rebecca P and Solomon Butler, Sept 12, 1792 (Sept 20?) %
Robert and Mary Tilton, Nov 21, 1793 %
[Silvanus and Jane Homes, July 1, 1725] *
Temperance of Tisbury and Matthew of Chilmark, Nov 29, 1798%
Tristram and Clarissa Mayhew, Dec 17, 1795 %
William of Chilmark and Love Coffin who was born Edgartown May 3 1756 - no marriage date # {not in church records}
Zebulon and Prudence Mayhew, May 7, 1789 %

ANDREWS, Josiah B, Capt, of Salem and Jane K Withington of Chilmark, May 26, 1819 *

ATHEARN, [Lydia of Tisbury and Capt Calvin C Adams, int Oct 10, 1835] % * [Lydia, sister to Zadoc] *
Polly and Nathaniel Mayhew m Feb 23, 1786 (Mary, Feb 20, 1784) %

ATHEARN, [Polly, d James and Rebecca (Scudder) Athearn *, and Nathaniel Mayhew, s Zaccheus and Rebecca (Pope) Mayhew] *
Samuel, of Tisbury and Susanna Adams, Apr 21, 1791 % *
[Samuel, s Jethro and Mercy (Chase) Athearn *, and Susanna d Mayhew and Rebecca (Mayhew) Adams] *
[Solomon and Sarah Skiff, July 24, 1717] *
Susanna, d Jethro, and Nathan Mayhew, June 28, 1761 (M)

BASSETT, [Cornelius, Col, and Lydia Norton, no date] *
[Ebenezer and Abigail Adams, May 21, 1780] * %
[Elizabeth and Thomas Smith, Sept 9, 1721] *
[Hope and Ebenezer Tisdale, Nov 12, 1730, Lebanon, Conn] *
[Mary and Benjamin Smith, Sept 23, 1716] *
Nathaniel Esq, s William and Anna, and Catherine Boardman, May 1, 1788 (May 2) %
Norton and Clarissa Stewart, Sept 22, 1791 (Sept 12/22) %
Polly and William Norton, Nov 10, 1769 %
William and Olivia Tilton, Nov 16, 1794 % * [to Zanesville OH 1806] *

[**BELCHER**, Moses Jr and Eunice Mayhew, March 18, 1736] *

[**BLAIN**, Mary and Thomas McGee, Nov 10, 1726] *

BOARDMAN, Catherine and Nathaniel Bassett Esq, May 1, 1788 (May 2) %
Andrew, Rev, and Catharine Allen, Oct 8, 1747 (M)
Walter and Jane Hillman, Dec 4, 1790 %

[**BOSWORTH**, ___ and Eliza Tilton, Aug 15, 1745] *

BROOKES (Crookes), Richard and Mary Chase, July 9, 1720(M)

BULLEN, Warren, Farmington ME, and Sally Mayhew, Sept 22, 1819 *

[**BURGESS**, Abigail and John Pease, May 24, 1739] *

BUTLER, Athearn and Desire Allen, Oct 2, 1788 %
David P and Martha Chase, both of Tisbury, Dec 15, 1846 (M)
Nicholas and Lucy Norton, Nov 5, 1789 %
Prudence and Shadrach Hillman, March 20, 1794 %
Rhoda and Moses Nye of Sandwich, Nov 11, 1793 % @

CHASE, [Alpheus and Miss Isabella Ferguson, Aug 14, 1850 in Chilmark, *Vineyard Gazette*] *
Isaac and Mary Pease, Apr 3, 1702 (M)
Lydia and Moses Hillman, Sept 11, 1794 %
Martha and David P Butler, both of Tisbury, Dec 15, 1846 (M)
Mary and Richard Brookes (Crookes), July 9, 1720 (M)

[**CHIPMAN**, Deborah and Nicholas Nickerson, May 2, 1722] *
[Hanaly and Jane Allen, April 24, 1740] *

CHURCHILL, William 3d of Plympton and Peggy Tilton, April 14, 1791 (April 14-21)%

[**CLAGHORN**, Thomas and Susanna Gibbs, Nov 2, 1732]*

CLARK, Ruth and Nathaniel Grennell, Nov 26, 1756 (M)
[Sarah and Capt John Gould, June 18, 1731] *

CODMAN, Hepsibah, d Robert, and Nathan Skiff, 1st wife c 1687 (M)

COFFIN, Love who was born Edgartown May 3 1756 and William Allen # (not in church records)

COFFIN, Matthew of Edgartown and Betsy Allen of Chilmark, Feb 21, 1799 %
[Prince and Mary Skiffe, Nov 10, 1727] *
Samuel, Capt, and Lucy Sprague, both of Edgartown, Oct 21, 1813

COLE, Anna and Joshua Johnson, int Nov 27, 1808 %, m Dec 6, 1808 {church rec: "Anna Cole, colored"}
John from New Bedford and Peggy Ryan of Chilmark, Oct 24, 1793 * [Rev Smith] *

COTTLE, Betsey and Seth Mayhew, June 4, 1801 (Elizabeth, 1801?)%
Cynthia and James Allen 2nd, int Aug 20, 1803 %, m Nov 15, 1803
Lot of Tisbury and Catherine Smith, Sept 30, 1804 %
Mayhew and Sarah Tilton, Dec 13, 1804 (Sary Tilton Jr) %
Polly and Joseph Mayhew of Falmouth, Oct 23, 1796 *
Rebecca and Joseph Green of Falmouth, July 4, 1813 *
Sarah and Mayhew Smith, int Mar 12, 1803 %, m Oct 27, 1803
Shubael Esq of Tisbury and Mrs Mary Allen, int May 26, 1803 %, m June 9, 1803
Silas and Jemima Tilton, Mar 19, 1795 %
William and Anna B Williams, Jan 23, 1806 %

[COVELL, Bethia and Jonathan Hillman, Feb 5, 1723] *

CROWELL, Jonathan of Tisbury and Remember Tilton, Apr 14, 1791 % *

[DAGGETT, Benjamin and Margery Homes, June 1, 1734] *
[Jacob and Hannah Skiff, Oct 24, 1714] *

DAVIS, Diadamia and Joseph Tilton Jr, Dec 25, 1788 (Deidamia) %

DAVIS, Rufus of Edgartown and Rebecca Mayhew, Dec 4, 1794 % {church records say she is sister to Chilmark William Mayhew}

DOANE, John and Lydia Thacher, both of Conn, June 10 {1708?} CTR

DUNHAM, Eleazer of Tisbury and Dinah Hillman, June 23, 1801 *
Polly and Matthew Tilton, Apr 1, 1806 % (church records say she was a Mayhew, widow of William Dunham, son of David)

[**ELISHA**, Elisha and Mary Steel, Jan 7, 1725] *

[**FERGUSON**, Miss Isabella and Alpheus Chase, Aug 14, 1850 in Chilmark, *Vineyard Gazette*] *

FISHER, Richard of Edgartown and Lydia West, Nov 1, 1799 (Nov 9) %

FLANDERS, Betsey and Cyrus Hatch, Sept 1, 1791 %
Elmira and Cornelius Tilton, Nov 21, 1816 *
John Jr and Hannah Tilton, Dec 23, 1792 %

FOLGER, Abishai and Sarah Mayhew [d Pain] *, Nov 6, 1727%*

[**GIBBS**, Susanna and Thomas Claghorn, Nov 2, 1732] *

GIFFORD, Elizabeth and Nathaniel Pease, Feb 21, 1796 %
Fear and Cornelius Robinson, April 20, 1792 (Apr 21)%

GLIFFORD, Rose and Fortunatus Pease Jr, Nov 28, 1788 (Gifferd) %

GODFREY, Patty and Archabald McCollum, Apr 24, 1800 %

GOULD, John, Capt, and Sarah Clark, June 18, 1731 *

GRAY, Freeman of Tisbury and Betsey Nichols, Oct 11, 1798 %
John of Tisbury and Mary Tilton 3rd, Feb 7, 1789 (no "3rd", Feb 17) %

GREEN, Joseph of Falmouth and Rebecca Cottle, July, 1813 *

GRENNELL, Nathaniel and Ruth Clark, Nov 26, 1756 (M)

HALLECK, Moses, Rev, of Plainfield, New Jersey, and Peggy Allen of Chilmark, Sept 12, 1792 (Hallock) %

[**HAMILTON**, Thomas and Jane McClellan, Oct 16, 1735] *

HAMMETT, Benjamin of Tisbury and Olive Hillman, Dec 1, 1791 %

HANCOCK, Juliana and Beriah Tilton, Sept 23, 1817
Philura (Philma?) and John Johnston of Tisbury, Dec 9, 1818

HATCH, Cyrus and Betsey Flanders, Sept 1, 1791 %
Nymphas, Rev, and Nancy Allen, April 22, 1802 * {church record: Nancy Allen, then "or Abigail" written above Nancy}
Reuben and Lucy Tilton, Dec 3, 1789 %

HAWKES, Fear and Thomas Tilton, May 17, 1805 (Hawks, May 11) %
Sylvia and Benjamin Richardson of Unity, Mar 24, 1791 (Hawks) % @

HILLER, Bethiah and Warren Waldron, 1839 (M)

HILLMAN, Dinah and Eleazer Dunham of Tisbury, June 28, 1801 *
Henry and Sarah Mayhew, Dec 9, 1790 (Sorah) %
Jane and Walter Boardman, Dec 4, 1790 %
[Jonathan and Bethia Covell, Feb 5, 1723] *
[Joseph and Keziah Norton, Nov 24, 1737] *
Lois and Daniel Look of Addison, Maine, Oct 7, 1804 % @
Moses and Lydia Chase, Sept 11, 1794 %
Nancy and Prince Hillman, July 18, 1801 %
Nancy, Mrs and Samuel Look Jr, int Mar 6, 1808 %, m Mar 27, 1808
Olive of Chilmark and Benjamin Hammett of Tisbury, Dec 1, 1791 % @
Parnell and Thomas Lumbert, Oct 30, 1791 %
Prince and Nancy Hillman, July 18, 1801 %
Prudence and Abraham Knowles, July 9, 1807 %
Rebecca and William Packard of Plymouth, March 8, 1815
[Sarah and Matthias Rogers, Oct 28, 1730] *
Shadrach and Prudence Butler, Mar 20, 1794 %
Silas Jr and Sukey Jones, Nov 25, 1798 (Nov 21)%
Stephen and Bathsheba Skiff, Apr 24, 1806 %
Tristram and Nabby Stewart, Sept 28, 1817 *
Uriel and Betsy Adams, Dec 21, 1797 %

[**HOMES**, Agnes and Joshua Allen, Dec 14, 1725] *
[Elizabeth and James Hutchinson, Feb 5, 1730 in Boston] *
[Jane and Silvanus Allen, July 1, 1725] *
[Katherine and Capt Samuel Smith, May 30, 1721] *
[Margery and Benjamin Daggett, June 1, 1734] *

[**HUNT**, William and Jane Tilton, June 2, 1718] *

[**HUTCHINSON**, James and Elizabeth Homes, Feb 5, 1730 in Boston] *

JOHNSON, Joshua and Anna Cole, Dec 6, 1809 (int Nov 27, 1808) {church records: "Anna Cole, colored"}
John of Tisbury and Philura Hancock, Dec 9, 1818 *

JONES, Sukey and Silas Hillman, Nov 25, 1798 (Nov 21) %

KING, Matthias and Mary Lock, Oct 28, 1736 *

KNOWLES, Abraham of Addison and Prudence Hillman, July 9, 1807 %

LAMBERT/LUMBERT, Bathsheba and William Pool, May 17, 1798 %
Belinda and Jeruel West of Tisbury, Dec 8, 1803 *
[Benjamin and Bathsheba Mayhew, Jan 16, 1735] *
Deborah of Chilmark and Isaac Winslow of Tisbury, Nov 20, 1800 % @
Deborah and Hayden Lumbert, Nov 26, 1818 *
Hayden and Deborah Lumbert, Nov 26, 1818 *
Laura and William Lumbert of Tisbury, June 6, 1811
Jonathan and Love Manter of Tisbury, Nov 19, 1800 %
Mary and Jeremiah Steward, Nov 6, 1788 (Stewart) %
Prudence and George West, Oct 27, 1796 *
Thomas and Parnell Hillman, Oct 30, 1791 %
William of Tisbury and Laura Lumbert, June 6, 1811

LAWRENCE, William of Falmouth and Hannah Allen, Nov 5, 1801 (Laurence)%

LOOK, Daniel of Addison, Maine and Lois Hillman, Oct 7 1804%
George of Tisbury and Persis Allen, Nov 27, 1800 %
[Jonathan and Mary Norton, Jan 1, 1730] *
Samuel Jr of Tisbury and Mrs Nancy Hillman, Mar 27, 1808 (int Mar 6)

[**LOTHROP**, Lydia and Thomas Mayhew, July 27, 1732] *

LUCE, Benjamin and Prudence Pease, Aug 14, 1791 (Benjamin Jr) %
Hannah and Mayhew Norton of Tisbury, July 6, 1797 % @
Jabez of Tisbury and Reliance Nichols Jr, Nov 5, 1802 (int Apr 3)
Richard, Capt, and Hepsibah Allen, Jan 9, 1817
Warren of Tisbury and Sally West, Oct 19, 1797 %

MAYHEW, [Abia and Benjamin Allen, Jan 8, 1730] *
[Abiah, d Thomas, and William Tilton, July 6, 1696] * (no date)%
Abner Jr and Eunice Smith, Nov 5, 1807 %
Allen, Dr, and Eunice Allen, Dec 18, 1795 %
[Bathsheba and Benjamin Lumbert, Jan 16, 1735] *
[Benjamin and Sarah Tilton, Aug 29, 1741] *
Betsey and Benjamin Skiff, Jan 26, 1820 *
[Betsey and Benjamin Hillman, Jan 26, 1820] * {ed note: possibly confused with entry immediately preceding}
Catherine Cottle [d Abner Jr and Eunice] and Capt Granville Manter *, int Oct 27, 1838 %
Clarissa and George Mayhew, Aug 25, 1817 *
Clarissa and Tristram Allen, Dec 17, 1795 %
Deborah and Abel Baker of New Sharon, Me, Aug 23, 1795 % @
[Dinah and Jethro Allen, Mar 25, 1736] *
Ephraim Jr and Susanna Pease, Feb 14, 1805 (Feb 13) %
Frederick and Zelinda Tilton, July 28, 1811 * [to Zanesville OH]*
George and Clarissa Mayhew, Aug 25, 1817 *
Hannah D and Oliver Mayhew, May 28, 1845 (M)
Harrison P and Susan Mayhew, Dec 14, 1820 *
Hebron and Rebecca Stewart, Sept 20, 1792 * (Deborah Stewart)%

MAYHEW, [Jedidah and Uriah Tilton, March 26, 1738] *
Jeremiah and Martha B Tilton, Dec 4, 1817 *
Jeremiah, Capt, of New Bedford, and Mrs Peggy Mayhew, Oct 26, 1792 %
Jonathan and Parnell Mayhew, Oct 25, 1792 %
Joseph of Falmouth and Polly Cottle of Chilmark, Oct 23, 1796 *
[Lucinda and Levi Davis, int Mar 2, 1827] * % [to Zanesville OH] *
[Martha and Shubael Smith Jr, Jan 23, 1723/4] * % (Shubil)
Mary and Ephraim Smith of New Sharon, Oct 2, 1800
Matilda and Elijah Smith, Aug 28, 1791 %
[Matthew and Mary [Skiff] *, March 1, 1674] * (Mary ___)
Matthew and Rebecca Stuart, 1779 (M)
Nathan and Susanna Athearn, d Jethro, June 28, 1761 (M)
Nathaniel and Nancy Allen, Dec 12, 1815 *
Oliver and Hannah D Mayhew, May 28, 1845 (M)
Parnell and Jonathan Mayhew, Oct 25, 1792 %
Peggy and Thomas Nickerson, Oct 3, 1816 *
Peggy, Mrs, and Capt Jeremiah Mayhew, Oct 26, 1792 %
Persis and Pain Tilton Jr, Sept 26, 1813 *
Polly m first William Dunham, s David; m 2nd Matthew Tilton, April 1, 1806
Polly and Ephraim Pool, Oct 18, 1804 % (church records: "Polly Mayhew, sister of Harrison P)
Prudence and Zebulon Allen, May 7, 1789 %
Rebecca and Capt Samuel Nickerson, Aug 15, 1817 *
Rebecca and Rufus Davis of Edgartown, Dec 4, 1794 % (church records: Rebecca, sister to Chilmark William)
[Reliance and Eliaship Adams, Feb 18, 1729]*
Ruhamah Jr and Benjamin Smith, Aug 22, 1793 *
[Ruth and Joseph Tilton, Nov 4, 1736] *
Sally and Warren Bullen of Farmington, Me, Sept 22, 1819 *
[Samuel and Love Norton, Dec 27, 1739] *
Sarah and Henry Hillman, Dec 9, 1790 (Sorah) %
Seth and Betsey Cottle, June 4, 1801 (Elizabeth) %

MAYHEW, Susan and Harrison P Mayhew, Dec 14, 1820 *
Susanna and Ransom Norton, March 27, 1791 %
[Thomas and Lydia Lothrop, July 27, 1732]*
Thomas W and Lucy Allen, Dec 23, 1810 *
William, Deacon, of Edgartown and Parnell Mayhew, Nov 23, 1820
William B and Prudence Allen, Nov 6, 1800 (William Brandon, Prudence Allen Jr)%
[Zaccheus, Col, and Susanna Wade of Ipswich] *
[Zachariah and Elizabeth Allen, Nov 21, 1738] *

[**MCCLELLAN**, Jane and Thomas Hamilton, Oct 16, 1735] *

MCCOLLUM, Archabald and Patty Godfrey, April 24, 1800 %

[**MCGEE**, Thomas and Mary Blain, Nov 10, 1726] *

MCKINSTRY, Moses and Louisa Robinson, Nov 16, 1820 *

MERRY, Lathrop of Tisbury and Abigail Pease, Dec 26, 1805 %@

[**MOORE**, David, Capt, and Kathren Allen, Aug 3, 1738] *

NICHOLS, Betsey and Freeman Gray of Tisbury, Oct 11, 1798 % @
Reliance Jr and Jabez Luce, int Apr 3, 1802 %, m Nov 25, 1802

NICKERSON, [Nicholas and Deborah Chipman, May 2, 1722] *
Samuel, Capt, and Rebecca Mayhew, Aug 15, 1817 *
Thomas and Peggy Mayhew, Oct 3, 1816 *

NORTON, [Content and John Thatcher, Nov 28, 1734] *
[Keziah and Joseph Hillman, Nov 24, 1737] *
[Love and Samuel Mayhew, Dec 27, 1739] *

NORTON, Lucy and Nicholas Butler, Nov 5, 1789 %
[Lydia and Cornelius Bassett, 1714] *
Lydia B and James N Tilton, July 2, 1837, int June 17 (M)
[Mary and Jonathan Look, Jan 1, 1730] *
Mayhew of Tisbury and Hannah Luce, July 6, 1797 %
Polly and Josiah Tilton, Nov 24, 1814 * (Mary B) %
Ransom and Susanna Mayhew, March 27, 1791 %
[Rebecca and Thomas Sturges, Feb 27, 1735] *
Thomas of Edgartown and Louisa Adams, Oct 26, 1806
    (Lovisa)%
Tristram and Polly B Tilton, Nov 25, 1813 *

NYE, [Elisha and Mehitabel Robinson, banns only 1776,
    DCHS]*
Moses of Sandwich and Rhoda Butler of Chilmark, Nov 11, 1792
    % @

PACKARD, William of Plymouth and Rebecca Hillman, Mar 8,
    1815 *

PEABODY, Peleg of Dartmouth and Sally Pease of Chilmark,
    Sept 8, 1799 (Pelig Peabarday) %

PEASE, [Abigail and Benjamin Skiffe, Sept 8, 1722] *
Abigail and Lathrop Merry of Tisbury, Dec 26, 1805 % @
Fortunatus Jr and Rose Glifford, Nov 28, 1788 (Gifferd) %
[John and Abigail Burgess, May 24, 1739] *
Mary and Isaac Chase, Apr 3, 1702 (M)
Nathaniel and Elizabeth Gifford, Feb 21, 1796 %
Persis and Anderson Taylor of Hallowell, Me, Jan 9, 1791 % @
Prudence and Benjamin Luce Jr, Aug 14, 1791 %
Sally and Peleg Peabody of Dartmouth, Sept 8, 1799 % @
Susanna and Ephraim Mayhew Jr, Feb 14, 1805 (Feb 13) %

POOL/POOLE, Ephraim and Lucinda Tilton, Jan 18, 1810 *
Ephraim and Polly Mayhew, Oct 18, 1804 %
Polly (Mary) and William West of Tisbury, March 23, 1809 * (int Nov 12, 1808) @
William and Bathsheba Lumbert, May 17, 1798 %

RICHARDSON, Benjamin of Unity and Sylvia Hawkes, Mar 24, 1791 %

ROBINSON, Anna and Ward Tilton Jr, Oct 16, 1812
Jedidah and David Tilton, Sept 25, 1806 %
John and Jane Allen, July 25, 1897 %
Louisa and Moses McKinstry, Nov 16, 1820 *

[**ROGERS**, Matthias and Sarah Hillman, Oct 28, 1730] *

RYAN, Peggy and John Cole of New Bedford, Oct 24, 1793 *

SKIFF/SKIFFE, Bathsheba and Stephen Hillman, Apr 24, 1806%
[Benjamin and Abigail Pease, Sept 13, 1722] *
Benjamin and Betsey Mayhew, Jan 26, 1820 *
[Hannah and Jacob Daggett, Oct 24, 1714] *
Joshua and Rebecca West, Nov 26, 1812 *
[Mary and Prince Coffin, Nov 10, 1727] *
Matty and David Tilton, Feb 27, 1800 %
Nathan and Hepsibah Codman, d Robert, 1st wife c 1687 (M)

SMITH, [Benjamin and Mary Bassett, Oct 23, 1716] *
Benjamin and Ruhamah Mayhew Jr, Aug 22, 1793 * (Ruhamah Tillton) %
Catherine and Lot Cottle of Tisbury, Sept 30, 1804 % @
Elijah and Matilda Mayhew, Aug 28, 1791 %
Ephraim of New Sharon and Mary Mayhew, Oct 2, 1800 %
Eunice and Abner Mayhew Jr, Nov 5, 1807 %

SMITH, Mayhew and Sarah Cottle, int Mar 12, 1803 %, m Oct 27, 1803
Sally and Asa Tilton, March 19, 1801 (Sarah) %
[Samuel, Capt, and Katherine Homes, May 30, 1721]*
Shubael and Deidamia Tilton, Sept 13, 1810 *
[Thomas and Elizabeth Bassett, Sept 9, 1721] *

SPAULDING, Sophia of Tisbury and Henry Allen, Feb 19, 1801%

SPRAGUE, Lucy and Capt Samuel Coffin, both of Edgartown, Oct 21, 1813

[**STEEL**, Mary and Elisha Elisha, Jan 7, 1725] *

STEWARD/STEWART/STUART
Clarissa and Norton Bassett, Sept 22, 1791 (Sept 22/12) %
Jeremiah and Mary Lumbert, Nov 6, 1788 %
Mary and William Tilton Jr, Sept 18, 1817
Nabby and Tristram Hillman, Sept 28, 1817 *
Rebecca {Stuart} and Matthew Mayhew, 1779 (M)
Rebecca and Hebron Mayhew, Sept 20, 1792 * (Deborah Stewart) %
William Jr and Bathsheba Tilton, Sept 17, 1789 %

STURGES/STURGIS, [John and Abigail Allen, Sept 5, 1728] *
[Thomas and Rebecca Norton, Feb 27, 1735] *

TAYLOR, Anderson of Hallowell, Me, and Persis Pease, Jan 9, 1791 % @
[Barnabas and Martha Allen, Oct 4, 1725]*

[**THACHER**, John and Content Norton, Nov 28, 1734] *
Lydia and John Doane, both of Conn, June 10 {1708?} CTR

[**TISDALE**, Ebenezer and Hope Bassett, Nov 12, 1730] *

TILTON/TILLTON, Asa and Sally Smith, Mar 19, 1801 (Sarah) %
Bathsheba and William Stewart Jr, Sept 17, 1789 (William Stewort) %
Beriah and Juliana Hancock, Sept 13, 1817 *
Cornelius and Elmira Flanders, Nov 21, 1816 *
David and Jedidah Robinson, Sept 25, 1806
David and Matty Skiff, Feb 27, 1800 %
Deidamia and Shubael Smith, Sept 13, 1810 *
[Eliza and Mr Bosworth, Aug 15, 1745] *
Eunice and Oliver Tilton, Jan 23, 1791 %
Francis and Parnell Tilton, Sept 13, 1812 *
Hannah and John Flanders, Dec 23, 1792 %
Hebron and Prudence Tilton Dec 26, 1811 *
James N and Lydia B Norton, July 2, 1837, int June 17 (M)
[Jane and William Hunt, June 2, 1718] *
Jemima and Silas Cottle, March 19, 1795 %
[Joseph and Ruth Mayhew, Nov 4, 1736] *
Joseph Jr and Diadamia Davis, Dec 25, 1788 (Deidamia) %
Josiah and Polly Norton, Nov 24, 1814 * (Mary B) %
Lucinda and Ephraim Poole, Jan 18, 1810 *
Lucy and Reuben Hatch, Dec 3, 1789 %
Martha B and Jeremiah Mayhew, Dec 4, 1817 *
Mary B and Tristram Norton {see Polly B} (M)
Mary Jr and Robert Allen, Nov 21, 1793 %
Mary 3rd and John Gray of Tisbury, Feb 7, 1789 (Mary, Feb 17)%
Matthew and Polly (Mayhew) Dunham, widow of William, April 1, 1806
Mercy and Thurston White, moved to Westport 1818 (M)
Oliver and Eunice Tilton, Jan 23, 1791 %
Olivia and William Bassett, Nov 16, 1794 %
Pain Jr and Persis Mayhew, Sept 26, 1813 *

TILTON/TILLTON, Parnell and Francis Tilton, Sept 13, 1812 *
Peggy and William Churchill of Plympton, Apr 14, 1791 (William 3d, Apr 14-21) @
Polly B and Tristram Norton, Nov 25, 1813 * {Cincinnati 1814(M)}
Prudence and Hebron Tilton, Dec 26, 1811 *
Rebecca and Samuel Tilton, Nov 9, 1815 *
Remember and Jonathan Crowell of Tisbury, April 14, 1791 % @
Samuel and Rebecca Tilton, Nov 9, 1815 *
[Sarah and Benjamin Mayhew, Aug 29, 1741] *
Sarah and Mayhew Cottle, Dec 13, 1804 (Sary Jr) %
Sophia and Matthew Vincent of Edgartown, Dec 21, 1809
Thomas and Fear Hawkes, May 17, 1805 (May 11, Hawks) %
[Uriah and Jedidah Mayhew, March 26, 1738] *
Ward Jr and Anna Robinson, Oct 16, 1812 *
William Jr and Mary Stewart, Sept 18, 1817 *
[William, s Samuel and Abiah Mayhew] % * [July 6, 1696] * (no date)
Zelinda and Frederick Mayhew, July 28, 1811 *

VINCENT, Matthew of Edgartown and Sophia Tilton, Dec 21, 1809

WALDRON, Warren and Bethia Hiller, 1839 (M)

[**WASS**, Wilmot and Rebecca Allen, March 22, 1733] *

WEST, George and Prudence Lumbert, Oct 27, 1796 *
Jeruel of Tisbury and Belinda Lumbert, Dec 8, 1803
Lydia and Richard Fisher of Edgartown, Nov 1, 1799 (Nov 9) @
Rebecca and Joshua Skiff, Nov 26, 1812 *
Sally of Chilmark and Warren Luce, Oct 19, 1797 (Salley) @
William of Tisbury and Polly Pool *, March 23, 1809 (Mary, int Nov 12, 1808)

WILLIAMS, Anna B and William Cottle, Jan 23, 1806 %

[**WING**, Elnathan and Hannah Allen, Oct 7, 1726] *

WINSLOW, Isaac of Tisbury and Deborah Lambert, Nov 20, 1800 %

WITHINGTON, Jane K and Capt Josiah B Andrews of Salem, May 26 1819 *

WORTH, William, Capt, Esq, of Edgartown and Martha Allen Jr, Sept 25, 1788 (Martha Allen, Apr 5, 1788)

DEATH ADDITIONS

ADAMS, Dinah, Oct 13, 1844, ae 80 yr (M)
James, Capt, ae 44, July 31, 1800, Panama fever [Savannah fever]
___, ch William Adams, d Dec 7, 1813
___, ch William Adams, d January 1815

ALLEN, Abigail, wid, July 12, 1806 %
Anna, ae 67, June 3, 1794 (Ann, wid John)
Beulah, May 28, 1806%
[Beulah Smith, w Samuel, ae 83, Mar 5, 1805]
Davis, s Eph, Aug 20, 1793, ae 15, mortification *
Deborah Gardner, wid Jonathan, Apr 19 1821 %
Desire, w Robert, June 13, 1792 (in 61st yr)
Frederick, s Henry and Sophia, Jan 2, 1806, ae 1 yr 9 mos %
George, Oct 1791
James, Dea, h Martha, Nov 3, 1815, ae 84, influenza %
Lucy, w Salathiel, Oct 18, 1793 *
[Moses, Feb 25, 1722] *
Patience, w Matthew, (Nov 6) 1797, ae 20
Peturah, (Pelnrah), d Josiah and Bathsheba, consumption, Apr 7, 1847, ae 73 %
Robert, h Desire, Jan 19 (Jan 10), 1801, ae 69 %
Sally (Sarah), Jan 23, 1812, ae 18 %
Samuel, ae 88, Oct 22, 1808 *
___, ch Zebulon, July 11, 1790
___, s Salathiel and Lucy, Nov 21, 1790, ae 6 dys
___, s Sylvanus, Jan 18, 1794, ae 12 hours
___, ch Sylvanus, Jan 4, 1795, just born
___, ch Sylvanus, 1797, ae 6 wks

ARMSTRONG, William, Feb 25, 1802 *

ATHEARN, Prince D, June 30, 1850, in California (M)

BASSETT, Catherine, w Nathaniel Esq, Mar 7, 1798, ae 46, apoplexy
Clement, 1798, at sea *
Cornelius, ca 1863, at Tarrytown NY *
Jane, w John, Apr 19, 1803 (ae 88y 7m) ae 89 %
John, (h Jane, ch Nathan and Mary) July 12, 1791, ae 85%
Martha, see Martha Williams
Martha, w Nathan, Nov 2, 1790 (in 35th yr), ae 34, delerium lunacy, lived 16 1/4 days without swallowing anything
Mary, wid, July 12, 1799 *, consumption
Nabby, Oct 25, 1808 ae 23 *, consumption
Nathan, Jan 15, 1792, ae 54, pleurisy *
Nathan, Rev, settled Charleston SC where he d June 26, 1738 *
Nathaniel, Esq, May 13, 1804 (Mar 13), in 77th yr %
Perez, 1796, in England *
Zipporah (Ziphorah), d Benjamin Esq and Abigail, Mar 16, 1812, of apoplexy

BOARDMAN, ____, twin of Walter and Jane, Sept 9, 1791
____, twin of Walter and Jane, Sept 9, 1791

BURGESS, Eliza, July 2, 1800 *
Shubael, Oct 11, 1798, ae 81, palsy *
____, wid, Oct 2, 1798, pleurisy *

BUTLER, [Daniel, May 5, 1735, at Chickasoo, Chilmark]
Elizabeth, 1802 [ae 93] *

CHASE, Isaac, Oct 13, 1716, drowned

[**CHIPMAN**, Mrs, Jan 29, 1726]

[**CLIFFORD**, Jon, Mar 28, 1728]

CLARK, ___, ch William, Dec 1814

COTTLE, Hannah, [Nov 18] 1797, ae 54 *
Jerusha, d Silas, Apr 10-14, 1790, ae 11 mos
Jerusha, w Silas, May 22, 1789 *
John, Feb 1804, ae 97
[Shubael, s James, Mar 18, 1722]

COX, Thomas, 1801 [at sea] *

DAGGETT, Jane, Feb 3, 1809 *
[Samuel, "a youth", Nov 14, 1717]
Solomon, July 23, 1797, ae 81 *

DUNHAM, Molly, June 5, 1811 *

FERGUSON, Mary, w John, Apr 6, 1810, ae 50

FISHER, Abiah, 1831 (M)

FLANDERS, Jane, d John and Sarah, Dec 27, 1790, ae 13,
    putrid fever *
Richard, s John and Sarah, Sept 20 1788, at sea, ae 14 *

GARDNER, Deborah, see Deborah Allen

GOFF, Lydia Ann, d William and Lydia, May 16, 1849, ae 3 yr
    HMP

HANCOCK, James, Aug 15, 1804, ae 37
___, ch Capt Samuel, June 1813

HATCH, Lucy, d Tryphena, Nov 17, 1794, diabetes [Samuel, May 13, 1739]
___, 1805, "delivery"

HAWKES, ___, Aug 2, 1815, ae 77, consumption

HILLMAN, [Abigail, d Richard, July 2, 1784]
[Benjamin, Apr 22, 1745]
[Bethia, June 21, 1727]
Ezra, Aug 2, 1810, ae 69, consumption *
Henry, Aug 21, 1798, yellow fever *
Isaiah, 1796, lost at sea *
James, Aug 9, 1819, ae 38 %
[John, Jr, Apr 21, 1728]
[Mary, June 21, 1727]
Molly, May 1816 *
Pardon, Oct 29, 1807, ae 20 % *
Prince, May 1802, at sea *
Rebecca, w Capt Robert, Oct 31, 1815, ae 70y 3m 11d, consumption %
[Richard, March 26, 1743, ae 68]
[Silas, June 11, 1727]
Silas, Dec 6, 1815, ae 84, consumption *
Walter, [Sept 15] 1797, lost at sea *
___, ch Edward, Feb 18, 1790
___, ch Thomas and Ruth, Mar 21, 1791, ae 1 day
___, ch Thomas, Oct 28, 1792

HOMES, Hannah, Mar 10, 1794, ae 85 *

HUNT, Mary, Mar 18, 1789, ae 68, bilious fever *

JONES, Daniel, h Mary, June 20, 1816, ae 77 (76y 3m 15d) %

JOHNSON, Adaline, Apr 17, 1843 (M)

LAMBERT, see LUMBERT

LATHROP, Sarson, Apr 7 1788, at sea, ae 20 *
Thomas, Capt, 1798, at Martinico *

LITTLE, [Thomas, early in 1715]
[Thomas, Dr, Mar 30, 1744]

LOOK, George, 1812 at sea *
Sarah, w Prince, Apr 18, 1800, ae 36, consumption %

LUCE, Sarah, Nov 5, 1797, ae 73 *
___, ch Ebenezer, Sept 1817
___, w David, Sept 4, 1818 *

[**LUKE**, Daniel, Apr 28, 1728]

LUMBERT/LAMBERT, Deborah A, w Hayden, June 1, 1819 (w
    Thomas H, May 31) %
Moses, Aug 2, 1819 *
Prudence, Sept 6, 1819 *
[Rachel, w Jonathan, Feb 13, 1734]
Thomas, Feb 10, 1815, lethargy, ae 49 *

MANTER, ___, ch Samuel, Oct 20, 1806 %

MAYHEW, Abiah, w Simon, Nov 3, 1792, ae 65 (in 64th yr),
    apoplexy %
Bethia, May 11, 1796 *
Elijah, May 30, 1788, nervous fever *
[Elijah, tailor, Dec 30, 1734]
Ephraim, h Jedidah, Oct 4, 1807, ae 62 (in 62d yr), mortification%

MAYHEW, Gideon, old age, Jan 1848 (1849?), ae 70 %
Hannah G, w John, Dec 17, 1801, ae 35 (in 35th yr), childbed %
Hilliard, ch Ephraim and Jedidah, Aug 11, 1817 (Aug 7), ae 25 (27th yr), apoplexy %
Jane, May 31, 1850 (M)
Jane, Miss, Apr 1849, ae 67 HMP=*Vineyard Gazette*/May 18, 1849 %
Jeremiah, Capt, June 14, 1790, ae 85 *
Jerusha, Dec 5, 1823, at Conway *
Jerusha, d Zephania and Bethia, Feb 23, 1793, ae 75 (Feb 22) %
Jethro, Oct 16, 1806, ae 55 (in 65th yr) %
John, Jan 16, 1790, ae 89 *
[John Sr, Mar 3, 1736, in 60th yr]
Jonathan, h Parnell, Dec 16, 1805 (Dec 7), in 52d yr, consumption %
Josias, Apr 30, 1799 *
Lois M, wid Capt Samuel, May 7, 1802 (May 8) %
[Lydia, old age, Aug 1848] %
Mark, Feb 9, 1814, ae 66, dropsy *
Mary, w Seth, Sept 12, 1800, ae 59, dysentery
Matthew, Dr, h Mary, Aug 10, 1805, ae 85 (in 85th yr) %
Mehitable, Mar 27, 1792, ae 85 *
[Nathan, s Capt Jeremiah and Deborah, Jan 14, 1760, ae 21y, 8 mos]
Nathan, Capt, July 26, 1800, ae 34, consumption (epilipsy) %
Nathan, Dea, March 25, 1791
Oliver, 1796 *
Pain, Jr, ch Pain and Mary, July 11, 1731 [drowned near West Chop]*
Parnel, wid Jonathan, Feb 10, 1808, ae 47, consumption %
Parnel, w Thomas, Mar 23, 1812, in 55th yr, cancer %
Patty, July 15, 1806, ae 17, consumption %
Peggy, w Capt Jeremiah, Sept 21, 1795, in 48th yr (2nd w Jeremiah, formerly w William) %

MAYHEW, Ruhamah, old age, (March 10, ?1849, ae 94) Miss, March 1-, 1849, ae 95 HMP %

Ruth, Dec 17, 1815, ae 94, influenza *

Samuel, Capt, h Lois, Apr 7, 1800, ae 88 (Apr 8) %

[Sarah, wid Thomas Esq, Dec 30, 1740 "she was 96" - Rev Homes]

Seth, h Mercy, Sept 20, 1800, ae 60y 5m 5d, dysentery %

Seth, formerly of Chilmark, Nov 1, 1850, in Delhi, Ohio, ae 79 HMP

Simon (h Abiah), (June 19) 1801 (in 82d yr) %

[Thomas, 2nd, s of Rev Thomas, b 1650, d July 21, 1715]

[Thomas, s Zacheus, May 26, 1745]

Thomas W, h Parnell, June 4, 1808, ae 52 (in 52d yr), consumption %

Tristram, ch Ephraim and Jedidah, Aug 1810, at Liverpool, England, smallpox %

Zachariah, Rev, (h Elizabeth) Mar 6, 1806, ae 89 %

[Zacheus, Col, h Susanna Wade of Ipswich, (h Rebeckah) Jan 3, 1760, in 76th yr] %

____, w Rev Zachariah, Mar 20, 1790, ae 69, pleurisy & consumption

____, stillborn ch Francis, July 11, 1790

____, ch John, July 1796

____, ch John, Feb 2, 1800, ae 1 month

____, ch Benjamin and Lydia, March 29, 1809 (inf s, March 19)%

____, ch Zephaniah, Dec 1810, ae 18, whooping cough

____, ch William B, June 15, 1817

____, ch David, Oct 15, 1819

MCCOLLUM, Hannah, Dec 4, 1808, ae 2y 7m, quinsy

____, ch ae 3 wks, Sept 20, 1810

NICKERSON, Abigail, wid, Feb 13, 1802, ae 82, palsy *

Jane, w Capt Samuel, Oct 8, 1815, ae 50y 3m %

NORTON, Betsy, June 12, 1809, dropsy *
Betsy, Sept 22, 1818, consumption *
Clement Bassett, s William and Polly, Apr 17, 1800, ae 6 mos
[Content, w Samuel Esq, Aug 2, 1839, in 63rd yr]
Elizabeth, w Capt Samuel, Sept 6, 1791, in 42d yr, consumption%
Jacob, Apr 13, 1793 (Apr 12), drowned coming from New Bedford, ae 53y 28d %
James, Apr 6, 1811, ae 57, consumption *
James, July 23, 1814 consumption *
[Jethro, May 12, 1743, ae 32]
Polly, Mar 25, 1813, consumption *
Rebekah, wid James, Apr 8, 1805, in 87th yr, dropsy %
Ruth, June 12, 1809, dropsy *
William, Mar 1, 1802 (Feb 28), ae 32, consumption %
____, ch William, Feb 5, 1805, ae 17 mos
____, twin s Samuel and Eunice, Aug 4, 1816 (Aug 3) %
____, twin s Samuel and Eunice, Aug 4, 1816 (Aug 3) %
____, Mrs, Dec 18, 1818, ae 94

PEASE, [Abigail, Mrs, May 2, 1741, in 80th yr]
Elizabeth, Sept 1, 1817, ae 79, consumption *
Polly, Nov 1806, dysentery %
Sarah, w Abisha, Nov 10, 1794, ae 63, dropsy *
Thomas, Oct 6, 1798 *
____, ch Fortunatus, Apr 15, 1795, ae 8 wks
____, ch Fortunatus, Aug 12, 1796 ae 7 wks
____, ch Nathaniel and Elizabeth, Sept 5, 1796, ae 4 wks
____, wid Fortunatus Pease Jr, Aug 4, 1798, consumption *
____, ch Nathaniel and Elizabeth, June 1803

PITTS, Thankful, wid, Mar 21, 1812, pleurisy *

POOLE, Benjamin, 1799, at sea *
Polly, (Mary) w Ephraim, Aug 30, 1806, in 27th yr %

POOLE, Martha, 1805, at sea *
Russell, ch of Nathaniel Esq, Jan 14, 1791, ae 3 dys
William, Oct 7, 1790, ae 49, atrophy *
____, ch of "Pool", Feb 7, 1819

REED, Lemuel B, of Dartmouth, Sept 23, 1848, 25y, typhus fever HMP

ROBINSON, Huldah, Oct 1832, res Pesque Island (M)
John, 1834 (M)
Silas, 1838, at Providence (M)

ROTCH, Francis, 23 Sept, 1848, ae ca 70 HMP

SKIFF/SKIFFE, [Abigail, Mar 4, 1739]
Matty, Apr 19, 1799, ae 44, consumption *
Nathan, May 1817, ae 89, consumption *
Remember, May 23, 1815, ae 100y 1m, dropsy
____, Oct 15, 1815, ae 54, dropsy

SMITH, Eunice, see Eunice Mayhew
Hannah, w Elijah, June 23, 1790, ae 42, consumption %
Matthew, s Elijah and Hannah, Oct 25, 1788, ae 1 yr
____, ch Mayhew, Sept 4, 1805, ae 1 yr

STEWART, Nabby, ch William and Bathsheba, ae 4, dysentery (no date)
William, ch William and Bathsheba, ae 2 yrs, dysentery (no date)
____, twin of William, Oct 27, 1798
____, twin of William, Oct 27, 1798

TILTON/TILLTON, Abiah, Sept 24, 1808, consumption *
Abigail, w Dr Tilton (w Dea Reuben), July 10, 1801, ae 59, consumption %

TILTON/TILLTON, Albert, Jan 20, 1814, typhus fever
Bathsheba, July 5, 1811, ae 49, inflammation of brain *
Cyrano (Sirano), ch John and Sarah, Feb 24, 1791 (Feb 23), ae 91 %
Daniel, h Lavinia, March 6, 1818 (March 7), ae 46y 1m 1d, dropsy %
[Deborah, d David and Jedidah, Sept 14, 1824]
Elizabeth, wid, Apr 17, 1803, ae 77 *
[Hannah, w Samuel, Apr 11, 1720]
Hellen, w Shadrach, June 27, 1849, ae 22 HMP
Isaac, Dec 28, 1815, ae 83, mortification *
[Jedidah, d David and Jedidah, Jan 10, 1826]
Jedidah, Miss, 5 Apr 1848, ae 89y 6m HMP
Jemima, w Isaac, Mar 13, 1810, ae 32, consumption *
[Jonathan, Feb 29, 1768, killed by lightning at Chilmark, ae 25, from *Boston Evening Post* 1768]
Joseph, Sept 3, 1796
Josiah, Esq, Mar 30, 1790 *
Levina, Feb 27, 1811, ae 35, dropsical consumption *
Levinthia, Apr 9, 1816, consumption *
Lydia, May 20, 1799, ae 23 *
Mary, wid, Sept 13, 1803, ae 87 *
Matthew Jr, Feb 7, 1805, ae 25, consumption *
Matty, w David, Jan 2, 1803, consumption
Moses, Jan 1817, at sea *
Nathan, Apr 1811, at sea
Nathan, Oct 30, 1819 *
Remember, w Cyrano, Nov 11, 1788, ae 86 *
Salathiel, Apr 1807, at sea *
[Samuel, s William, Feb 24, 1722]
[Samuel, Nov 29, 1731, ae 93]
Sarah, w Matthew, July 2, 1805 (July 3), in 52d yr %
Stephen, May 9, 1813
Susan, w Benjamin S, Mar 7, 1849 (Mar 8), dropsy of heart, ae 51 HMP %

TILTON/TILLTON, Susan, w Pain, July 1818, fever *
Uriah, Jan 1, 1785, ae 74
William, Sept 12, 1816, ae 77, consumption [Apr 12, 1816] *
Zedidah, wid of Uriah, Mar 31, 1788, ae 69
Zeno, s Daniel and Lavinia, Nov 4, 1817, at sea (Nov 1, on return voyage from South Sea), ae 18y 10d %
Zilpha, w Joseph, Feb 18, 1810 (1809), ae 88 %
____, ch William Jr, April 1793, ae 4 dys
____, ch Ward and Betsy, Sept 13, 1796, ae a few hours
____, ch Ezra, Jan 4, 1801, ae 18 mos
____, ch Oliver, Dec 22, 1806, ae 14 mos
____, ch David, Aug 2, 1817, ae 2 yrs, worm fever

WEEKS, Jesse, Apr 13, 1800, ae 87 *
Nathan, Dec 29, 1790, ae 78, atrophy *

WEST, Sarah, w Capt Thomas, Feb 1816 (Jan 31), consumption%
Thomas, Capt, 1807 [1806] (Nov 1816), lost at sea % *
____, d Thomas, July 9, 1790, ae 14 mos

WILLIAMS, Martha S, Mrs, w of Samuel, d Jonathan Bassett, formerly of Chilmark, ae 30, Nov 30, 1850, at Stors, Ohio HMP

WINSLOW, Huldah R, w James, d Amassa Gifford, June 23, 1846, ae 21 yrs (M)

WYER, Hannah, Oct 22, 1802 *